Praise for *Get Signed*

"All aspiring authors know the value of a great literary agent, but few know how to get one. Lucinda Halpern has written the definitive guide to attracting an agent and laying the groundwork for a book well worth publishing."

— **Adam Grant**, #1 *New York Times* best-selling author
of *Think Again* and *Hidden Potential*

"While Lucinda Halpern offers invaluable advice for navigating the choppy waters of literary agencies and publishing houses, she does something even more valuable with *Get Signed*. She entices the writer to elevate the storytelling, to create a timeless book, and to launch a dream career."

— **Jenny Jackson**, vice president and executive editor at Alfred A. Knopf and *New York Times* best-selling author of *Pineapple Street*

"Lucinda Halpern and her book are the map and the compass for any beginning writer looking for a way to find their perfect agent. There is no question in my mind that it will forever be the only book anyone trying to break into publishing will ever need. If only I had it when I was starting out! Wherever Lucinda leads, I will follow."

— **Sam Wasson**, *New York Times* best-selling author
of *Fosse, The Big Goodbye,* and *Fifth Avenue, 5 A.M.*

"Step by clear, insightful step, Lucinda Halpern gifts writers with the knowledge of what an agent does and how the writer-agent partnership works. She offers concise steps and exercises to help ready writers present their best ideas with excellent writing and secure platforms. As the title promises, this is the book to read to get signed."

— **Marion Roach Smith**, author of *The Memoir Project*

"Lucinda Halpern offers aspiring authors a step-by-step, actionable road map for landing a literary agent. She pulls back the curtain to show you the nitty-gritty details agents and publishers are looking for so you can nail your big idea, dial in your pitch, and present yourself as the best author for the job. Full of insider wisdom suitable for writers of every genre, *Get Signed* gives you just what you need to woo—and then wow— the agent of your dreams. Highly recommended!"

— **Kelly Notaras**, author of *The Book You Were Born to Write*

"In this indispensable book, Lucinda Halpern teaches authors how to meet the marketplace and the moment. She turns overwhelm into action steps and helps make publishing dreams come true."

— **Nicola Kraus**, #1 *New York Times* best-selling co-author of *The Nanny Diaries*

GET SIGNED

Find an Agent,
Land a Book Deal,
and Become a Published Author

LUCINDA HALPERN

HAY HOUSE, INC.
Carlsbad, California • New York City
London • Sydney • New Delhi

Published in the United States by: Hay House, Inc.: www.hayhouse
.com° • *Published in Australia by:* Hay House Australia Pty. Ltd.: www
.hayhouse.com.au • *Published in the United Kingdom by:* Hay House
UK, Ltd.: www.hayhouse.co.uk • *Published in India by:* Hay House Publishers India: www.hayhouse.co.in

Cover design: David Drummond
Interior and cover layout: Bryn Starr Best

Library of Congress Cataloging-in-Publication Data

Names: Halpern, Lucinda, author.
Title: Get signed : find an agent, land a book deal, and become a published author / Lucinda Halpern.
Description: 1st edition. | Carlsbad, California : Hay House, Inc., 2024.
Identifiers: LCCN 2023045080 | ISBN 9781401975142 (trade paperback) | ISBN
  9781401975548 (ebook)
Subjects: LCSH: Authorship--Vocational guidance. | Authorship--Marketing.
Classification: LCC PN153 .H35 2024 | DDC 808.02--dc23/eng/20231010
LC record available at https://lccn.loc.gov/2023045

Tradepaper ISBN: 978-1-4019-7514-2
E-book ISBN: 978-1-4019-7554-8
Audiobook ISBN: 978-1-4019-7555-5

10 9 8 7 6 5 4 3 2 1
1st edition, February 2024

Printed in the United States of America

This product uses papers sourced from responsibly managed forests.
For more information, see www.hayhouse.com.

To writers everywhere,

and to Patty Gift

CONTENTS

AUTHOR'S NOTE

Throughout this book, you will find several industry-specific words in bold italic. A glossary defining these terms is included at the back of this book for your reference.

At GetSignedBook.com you can find our master classes, free trainings, and more ways to help you toward your goal of becoming a published author.

INTRODUCTION

Here's How You Crack the Code to Book Publishing

"How do I get a literary agent?" Because agents hold the key to getting published, it won't surprise you that this is the question I have encountered most often in my career. In my inbox, at conferences, and even out for cocktails, it's the one thing every writer wants to know. Unfortunately, "I can't even get a response!" usually comes next. It's an increasingly common refrain.

If you've picked up this book because you want to know what it takes to break through to agents, editors, and readers, you've come to precisely the right place to get answers. Many of you are writing a manuscript or book proposal, and you're thinking about the next step. Maybe you have self-published or queried for months and, painfully, are not receiving any traction. Or maybe you are reentering the marketplace, having been published years ago.

No matter where you are in the journey, I have a plan that will guide you to becoming a recognized author. Whether you're writing a parenting book, a business book, a novel, a biography, a memoir, a book of humor, self-help, or inspiration, everything here is applicable to you.

Getting signed by a literary agent is more crucial to success in the book business than ever before. As bookstores dwindle and shelves overflow with blockbuster bestsellers from already-established authors, the playing field has never been so crowded for new authors trying to break in. If you want a book deal, you'll want an agent, because in this competitive landscape, publishers bet on what's already been proven to succeed. Most publishers will not even accept unsolicited queries from writers. They count on agents to be their gatekeepers.

Literary agents are first and foremost dealmakers. We look to protect your fiduciary interests and intellectual property rights and ensure that you get your money's worth. But we're more than that. The best of us aren't just brokering a single deal—we're in it for the duration of your career. As equity partners, we are only successful if you are.

For nearly 20 years, as a publicist, then a literary agent, and finally as the owner of the boutique agency Lucinda Literary, I've guided books to publication with top publishing houses and onto bestseller lists. At our agency, when we sign a new author, we're never just thinking about book one. We're thinking about books two and three and how those books can elevate and expand an author's career.

Because there are patterns to success, I've assembled the blueprint. For all the things I have said a thousand times to my clients, I found a shorthand that I hope will make the key points accessible to you.

Publishing doesn't have to be mysterious—shrouded in secrecy, its doors long locked to outsiders. Unfortunately, because there is so much need for information, a lot of misinformation exists that demoralizes writers, thwarting their chance at success. This advice is not only dangerously wrong in most instances, but it's confusing, and much of it is outdated, subjective to the agency or publisher, and espoused by authors and coaches, not the industry gatekeepers who make the decision every day of whether to take on a new writer. Most have not been in the trenches of New York bookselling, meeting with editors or pitching to the media. But it's time to change the message and bust all the myths out there. While it can help, you don't need to have a connection to New York or with anyone in the publishing industry. You don't have to have an advanced degree or millions of social media followers. And plenty of agents take on first-time authors.

Agents are people like you. Books have always mattered profoundly to us, just as they have to you. Many agents began their careers as English majors and aspiring authors.

MY STORY

Long before I became a literary agent, I too wanted to be a writer. Leaving my home and family behind in New York at 22, I rented a sofa in my friend's Parisian garret apartment. I walked along the perimeter of the Seine and drank espressos by day. By night, I wrote poetry and journaled hopeful memoirs. But six months later, my dream to publish a book had not materialized (just yet!), and I returned to Manhattan to take a position with HarperCollins as a book publicity assistant. In my daily work, I communicated with various media outlets—newspaper and magazine editors, radio and television producers—and coordinated book tours. I found that I not only related to the ever-querying minds, ambitions, and insecurities of the authors with whom I worked, but I also loved to fight for them, tooth and manicured nail.

I learned that books don't simply sell themselves and that having the right partner is invaluable. I fantasized about what it would be like to sculpt and promote a book on its rise to stardom before the world knew its name. And that's when I learned about the role of a literary agent, a position that united a passion for craft and communication with an appetite for business.

Unlike any other job I knew of, this one had my name on it. And despite having no experience, I was determined to find my way in. I knocked on every door in Manhattan until I found one agent willing to take a chance on me. (In my work with writers today, I am reminded of this experience often—all the frustration of rejection, followed by the thrill and validation the moment I found "my" person, the one who believed in me. I tell writers like you every day: It just takes one.) As a marketing consultant at that agency, I had the opportunity to work with authors like Gretchen Rubin and I began building a client list of my own. Then, at 27, I decided to start my own company.

Lucinda Literary was intended to be a "new media boutique," one that recognized the value of online marketing early on and helped authors utilize it, blending literary representation and publicity. I was hungry and scrappy, making phone calls when the phone wasn't ringing, reading every query in my inbox, and mining for talent wherever I could find it. Did you know that most gatekeepers in publishing will sign new talent from out of our inboxes? Every single agent and editor I interviewed for this book still does, even many years into their careers. That's what an outstanding pitch can do.

But a pitch isn't all that matters. This book is about building the right foundation for your book so the pitch becomes incredibly easy.

HOW TO USE THIS BOOK

In these pages, I will break down the process of pitching and acquiring a literary agent—no holds barred—so you can realize the dream of getting a book published. This is the dream that many of you have only talked about, for far too long, until now.

Get ready to discover a framework for acquiring an agent in just six steps. I call it the "Author Road Map." It's the result of nearly two decades spent dissecting everything I have learned from the nuances of this industry. In the chapters ahead, I'll divulge the famous names and little-known stories of authors who began just like you. *Book editors* of major publishing houses and top-tier agent colleagues will also share their wisdom about the first-time authors they signed and the pitches that made them sit up and pay attention.

In **Step 1: Discover Your Big Idea**, you'll learn how to land on the right concept for your book. Whether you're writing fiction or nonfiction, your approach needs to be both timely and timeless, as relevant today as it will be years from now. You want to build a foundation for an enduring book, not just one that can get a deal. It can take time to discover and refine your concept. Often it requires research, conversations, and keen observation. The best ideas contain universal themes but also a unique angle. This can feel like a fine line to walk, but I have developed a system to tell you when you've got it right.

Next we turn to **Step 2: Decide Your Differentiator**. After you have your big idea, you need to know where it fits in the publishing landscape and how to define your audience. This is what we call learning the market. As you delve into Step 2, I'll take you inside the brain of a literary agent who will later pitch your book to editors.

It all begins with understanding what we call comps and how they can work to your advantage. Here, your work is to envision your book's success by striking the chords of both the popular and the new, proving that there's a demand for your book.

In **Step 3: Pinpoint What Your Reader Craves**, you'll discover the most important thing that successful authors have—a clear answer to the question: Who is this book for? The answer isn't "everyone." Good writers understand that the best way to write for a specific reader is to know what they want from you. Why would they pick up your book? Do you solve a problem, delve deep into a topic of interest, or simply entertain and delight? The best authors do all three for their readers, and agents expect a clear (and research-backed) explanation of who you write for and what your book offers.

As you start down the road to publishing, you will need to step into your authority. In other words, why are you the best person to write this book? What makes you the best messenger for your big idea? This is where many writers get stuck. In **Step 4: Claim Your Authority**, I'll explain how to convince agents of your authority by identifying the one thing you do best and letting it shine.

For **Step 5: Get Seen**, we'll dive into the word of the day in publishing: *platform*. Does it matter? Do you need one? The short answer is yes. But don't be intimidated—there are many ways in which agents consider your platform, and they differ among categories and genres. Even for those who are seasoned marketers or excited about promotion, the book world can be specific as to how your platform is evaluated. I'll show you why you should feel confident in your own potential and how you can leverage your best assets to get seen.

A brief "intermission" reveals exactly how the strengths you've discovered will make you successful as I take you through **The Four Kinds of Writers Who Get Book Deals**. In my experience, there is a unique set of traits that predispose writers to winning an agent and a publishing contract, which can be sorted into four types. I'll help you determine which kind you are, so you can highlight your strengths and use every asset to your advantage.

In **Step 6: Pitch Persuasively**, we combine everything you've learned to create a captivating elevator pitch and write your query letter. This is what you will submit to agents to introduce them to you and your big idea. Think of your pitch like a movie trailer, a first look, an invitation to a conversation. The best thing you can do to increase your chance of landing a literary agent? Nail your pitch. I'll teach you how to make yours irresistible to get the response you deserve.

> A query letter is a brief e-mail to introduce yourself and your book to a literary agent. It has one purpose: to seduce them into requesting to read your work, with the ultimate goal of representing it.

Once you have a stellar pitch in hand, it's time to **Find Your Agent**. I will teach you how to research, sleuth, and choose the best literary agent for you. Because this will be a key relationship to your career, and a long-standing one, before you begin your outreach, you need to understand how the relationship truly works. Once you have found your match, I'll show you how to close the deal, providing you with the critical questions to ask and signs to look for to ensure you're making the right choice.

This book reveals the blueprint I have seen work time and again and the one I have taught to hundreds of writers to achieve their ultimate goal of becoming an author. Every step of the way, you will find easy prompts and memorable takeaways that you can put into practice immediately.

Your dream to get published is well within your reach, and it starts with finding the right literary agent to partner with. You are here to get signed. And I can't wait to get you started.

THE PROCESS OF GETTING AN AGENT

START HERE

An Author's Secret Weapon

First, a primer: What exactly does a literary agent do?

The cursory answer is that we make deals, but the truth is more comprehensive. We are developers and producers and partners. Agents can elevate the fee you receive for your book to numbers you never imagined possible and would be unlikely to obtain on your own. But the most gratifying thing I hear from clients as we scream together on the phone over an astonishing sales figure or book deal is this: "Thank you for advocating for the vision I had for my book all along. You always saw it, and you honored it."

Simply put, agents assemble the best product, people, and publishing experience possible for authors. In just a few pages, we'll dive into the four primary ways an agent achieves this.

EDITORIAL DEVELOPMENT

The best agents will work with you in a hands-on, collaborative way to make sure your book is speaking to its reader and the market at large. The greatest value we can lend is a big-picture critique, guiding you to think about your book more commercially. Peter Heller, the best-selling author of *The Dog Stars* and *The River*, puts it this way: "My agent is my sounding board who can help me with the story when I'm having challenges, who appreciates the language and the characters and just has brilliant ideas about how to solve problems in the book."

Many first-time authors are under the impression that once they've acquired an agent, querying publishers begins almost simultaneously with a book deal essentially guaranteed. In a perfect world, that might be true, but the reality is that your ***manuscript*** will likely need additional shaping by your agent before it is sent to an editor. You may be tempted to send it too early, before it's ready; we'll keep your urgency at bay until it is. Or you may be so perfection-driven that you never see it as finished. Agents live by the philosophy of "done, not perfect." We can tell you when your proposal or manuscript is ready and ensure you submit your best work. Your ***material*** may even need additional revisions if a contract isn't secured at first ***submission***. (In Step 6, you will find a realistic timeline for your book's submission and ultimate publication.)

INDUSTRY RELATIONSHIPS

Literary agents have spent years establishing trust with editors. Our e-mails elicit quick responses. Once your agent has determined that your manuscript (for fiction) or ***book proposal*** (for nonfiction) is ready to be submitted to editors, an agent's industry relationships become crucial.

We prize speed and efficiency in our submissions at Lucinda Literary, "soft pitching" editors in conversations well before they see a proposal to solicit early constructive feedback. If the pitch is strong enough to linger in their minds, they will be all the more primed to receive it when the time comes. Publishers will either respond enthusiastically or they won't. The feedback from editors who don't ultimately acquire your book can be a gift to authors. We also see it as vital in refining the package, framing the book in just the right way later in the process to receive the best market reception.

> A book proposal is submitted by agents to prospective editors (before you write the book) and makes the business case for why your book is marketable. It is only required for nonfiction.

Well-connected agents will curate a submission list of editors with whom they have established relationships, even close friendships, at publishing houses. (In fact, when an experienced agent is intrigued by a pitch at the outset, a list of editors comes to mind immediately.) Our edge is the mutually beneficial relationships we've created. But make no mistake: your agent works for you, and your editor works for the publisher. These relationships are church and state. I'm never afraid to be blunt with a publisher if my author deserves more consideration. It is an agent's job to advocate for their client's interests. A good agent does so with fairness and respect.

CONTRACT NEGOTIATION

When an agent represents you as an author, your book's value immediately increases in the eyes of publishers. That's just human psychology combined with business understanding. And to your benefit, agents work "on spec" (speculatively, without a guarantee) for however long it takes to secure a contract. Only then do we receive a standard percentage—at the time of writing this book, a 15 percent commission in perpetuity.

Many writers I meet are so honored and elated to receive a book contract in the first place, they sign on the dotted line without asking a single question, worried they will lose a deal if they press for anything at all. This can be a huge mistake! The first offer could quite possibly be low or have a flat-fee structure when you might have been able to get an *advance*. Perhaps the royalty percentage the publisher grants is less than standard, you give away rights that you're actually entitled to, or you inadvertently agree to pay back your fee or advance if your book is canceled or the agreement is terminated. Did you also note how you're protected if a legal proceeding ensues, what happens if your book goes out of print, or whether you are beholden to the publisher for your next book?

With an agent as your advocate and negotiator, a $30,000 offer for worldwide rights of your book, including film rights, could increase to a $50,000 offer for North American print rights alone, with an additional $15,000 for audio rights, $40,000 for translations overseas, and a film option that, if developed, could bring your income to seven figures. Aren't you glad you didn't sign that initial contract?

Getting more money than you thought possible is exciting, without a doubt. But having an airtight contract that protects your interests may be even more important in the long term. Whether your book sees great success or is published in a way that disservices it, the legal implications can be countless and confusing. An experienced agent is looking out for these scenarios and will make sure you are duly rewarded for a positive outcome while protecting you in case of a negative one.

PARTNERSHIP AND ADVOCACY

Good agents oversee every move the publisher makes with discernment so that your book receives the best possible treatment, the largest distribution, and therefore the greatest chance of finding widespread success. A good agent stays in it with you long after the deal, advising on everything from your book cover design to media plans to much, much more. Because we take care of the uncomfortable conversations and chase the payments, you are left to have an unmuddled and creative relationship with your editor. We manage the project managers, so to speak.

We also troubleshoot if something goes awry in the relationship with your publisher. For example, let's say you delivered a partial manuscript six weeks ago but haven't had any communication from your editor, your jacket isn't what you hoped for at all, or the publicity team is silent. In each of these instances, you can enlist your agent to advocate for your needs.

Now that you understand all the ways in which an agent can serve you beyond selling your work, let's dive into the first step to acquiring an agent. It's time to discover your big idea.

STEP 1

Discover Your Big Idea

Dear Lucinda,
I have a book idea, but how do
I know if I'm even on the right track?

— MICHELLE (IOWA CITY, IA)

There are three keys to getting an agent and a subsequent book deal.

1. A big and bold idea

2. Excellent writing

3. An undeniable platform

Here's some encouraging news: you only need two of the three to succeed. All three would be fantastic, but only two are required.

In this step, we're going to uncover the first key. Every book starts with an idea. But many of these ideas will be seen by publishers as "small." In the language of agents and editors, a good idea is a *big* idea. But what does that mean? Why would any idea be "small"? And how do you know if yours is big enough?

This is the first metric you have to get right. I can solve a lot of problems for my authors, but if their idea doesn't work, I can only do so much to dress up the pitch. To discover your big idea, there are proven tactics that will command the attention of a literary agent. It may take trial and error, but you don't have to shoot in the dark! In the next few pages, I will walk you through exactly how to evaluate and tweak your idea to ensure it makes the impact you want it to with agents, publishers, and readers.

~~

I can't tell you how many writers come to me believing they had a specific book to write and eventually learn that they were wrong—happily in the end. CEOs, scientists, and leaders of all kinds struggle with the vulnerable and humbling process of putting themselves on the page, unsure if they are saying anything of value. Often these writers are a mix of confident in themselves or in their careers but self-doubting and anxious as they enter this entirely new arena, understanding that there is so much they do not know. Once these accomplished individuals realize that they do have a message or story worth sharing, there's an unexpected liberation. What's more: the most promising idea is the one you overlooked because it seemed too natural, simple, or easy.

Take Serena Quaglia, my first coaching student, who came to me wanting to write a novel. As a commercial real estate executive, she was accomplished in her field and set forth to achieve her dream of publishing with the same drive and determination she had with everything in her life. Her novel, drawing from her personal experience as a professional dancer in Las Vegas, showed promise and thrill. But she couldn't get an agent to read it. The dream that she had harbored since childhood was on life support. Why couldn't she succeed?

When I first met Serena over Zoom, I could see how lost and overwhelmed she was by the conflicting information she had researched. I felt compelled to ask: "How are you sure that this is the book you were meant to write?"

To this, she looked bemused. She answered that she honestly didn't know. Over several sessions, I learned that Serena had grown up in a small Kansas town with nothing to her name, survived breast cancer, and risen to the top of her field twice. She had so much to offer by way of advice! Her passion and expertise were palpable, and most of all, she had empathy. Essentially, she had every marking of a great self-help author.

As soon as I realized this, I told Serena, "I think you're a role model for younger women who have had to work their way to the top and who have faced obstacles at every turn, just like you. You deeply understand what these women are missing in their lives because you work with them every day. You can speak well to their challenges."

In our sessions together, I had never seen Serena emanate such radiance as she did in that moment. I encouraged her to let go—break free from whatever prestige she associated with writing a novel—and share all of the wisdom she had learned, the wisdom organic to her that would help so many others.

There is a magic that happens when you land on the idea that you are uniquely positioned to write. When you tap into that confidence, agents will see it.

TAKE YOUR IDEA FROM SMALL TO BIG

Landing on the first key, the right concept, can take experimentation and time, but there are parameters to follow that will tell you if you've truly discovered your big idea, one that grabs an agent at first read. Mining for it is an art, but it is also a science. You are laying the strong foundation that will shape everything that follows.

The two necessary conditions for a big idea are:

1. It has a universal theme and a unique point of view.

2. It is timely and timeless.

Your whole career trajectory can change when you understand this. It is the simplest way to get at the essence of your message, and for nonfiction authors, you'll find that it will inform, and then transform, your brand and your business.

You may have entered the world of books because you've always loved reading and writing or dreamed about becoming an author since childhood. But go deeper. Why did you decide to write a book? Your idea begins with you, but it must be bigger than you.

Did you encounter a challenge and look for a resource to guide you but couldn't find one? Or is there a topic you always wanted to immerse yourself in to learn more about? Or maybe, as a novelist, you couldn't stop fantasizing about a particular plot or set of characters? Your "why" for writing your book is knowing the end effect you want to have on a reader.

Your big idea is not the outline of your book but rather the core message that it brings to light. Ready for some tough love? The book idea you're considering or actively pitching to agents is probably too small. It's one of the most common mistakes. And agents and editors will pass on an idea that's seen as "familiar" or "niche" (aka "small"). Here are some real examples from the *slush pile* that we see regularly:

- Memoirs about healing based on a person's life story, devoid of other characters or themes

- The overly done and derivative self-help book empowering us to be "authentic" without a novel observation or uncommon method

- Biographies or histories of a person or time period not well known, without a compelling reason why this particular story has contemporary appeal

- Novels (whether in romance, fantasy, mystery, or other genres) without a surprising twist or stand-out character

- Business books that lean too heavily on memoir and promote the same "how-to" principles without any fresh insights

Your book will need to contribute something new to the category or conversation, and that quality of differentiation is what truly makes a book stand out. But don't despair; big ideas often start small. Here's how they can grow.

Universal Theme + a Unique Point of View

An engaging concept is born of a universal theme as old as time—such as love, loss, health, affliction, money, or relationships—and fashioned with a unique point of view.

First let's focus on how to assess whether your theme will resonate. In order to succeed in the marketplace and strike a chord with anyone who reads your book, the idea driving it must capture a reader's mind with something widely felt or understood.

A universal theme applies to nonfiction and fiction alike but is often most easily identified in memoirs, so let's look to them as an example. Successful memoirs aren't just about someone's personal story—they touch on something larger. Maybe this is pain, romance, nature, spirituality, or a combination.

When I spoke with Tracy Sherrod, a vice president at Hachette, one of the **Big Five** publishing houses, she relayed this sentiment: "When [a memoir is] too personal, too insular, and doesn't bring in the broader world, that, to me, is a mistake. You have to have something that makes people care." It's an important point. Readers are always wondering subconsciously: *What's in it for me?* Your story can transfix them when you include a sweeping theme that applies to many people, not just those you know.

In addition to a comprehensive theme, spinning your story in a new way that speaks to the current moment but can stand the test of time is a proven combination. "Tell me something I don't know about a subject I love," I've heard one of my agent colleagues say. In other words: contribute something new to what's already been said, and you will claim your seat at the table.

Adam Grant, the best-selling author of *Give and Take* and *Think Again*, suggests thinking this way about it: "In nonfiction, having a topic that's interesting and important isn't enough. You also need to have something distinctive to say. The ideal first book is one where your personal expertise and experience give you a novel perspective on an issue that readers find fascinating and consequential."

I love that word: *consequential*. Readers are unlikely to pick up any book where the stakes don't feel high—whether it's a matter of their own survival or the survival of a fictional character. An editor can easily spot a book that matters.

Fiction writers are not exempt from this formula. My client Jayne Allen, who you'll hear from a few times in this book, wrote the novel *Black Girls Must Die Exhausted*. Jayne's characters grappled with race, infertility, and loss, but with a healthy dose of levity. Her novel broke through because over the course of her research, she identified a hole in the market for depictions of contemporary Black women tackling difficult but common realities with a balance of joy and humor.

For self-help authors, my client Dan Martell offers a different example. Well known in the software world, Dan regularly coaches CEOs, entrepreneurs, and high performers in his industry. "Business owners I coach have trouble letting go," he told me in pitching his idea. "They're burned out because they try to do everything. They wish they could clone themselves. They can't." To solve this chronic and universal challenge, Dan developed a framework to *buy back your time*.

This might not seem too exciting at first. Isn't that just another take on delegation? Pretty standard advice, right? But Dan's idea had a unique pivot. His recommendation was that CEOs do only 5 percent of what they do really well and do it all the time. In fact, he advised that 95 percent of your current job is busywork and should be outsourced. Now that's pretty radical.

Here's the biggest clue to whether your concept is as big as we need it to be: it's unexpected or counterintuitive. At my agency, we're always looking for the surprise twist in a pitch. Suggesting that CEOs quit doing 95 percent of what they currently do is remarkable, even groundbreaking. Publishers found Dan's angle exciting, easily digestible, and memorable enough that the book attracted an auction and major deal with Penguin Random House. When it launched, *Buy Back Your Time* quickly hit multiple bestseller lists.

Something similar happened with Dr. Marisa Franco's book *Platonic: How the Science of Attachment Can Help You Make—and Keep—Friends*. Marisa didn't have a huge platform (a concern of many aspiring authors and one we'll address in Step 3) when she received an offer from Michelle Howry, an executive editor at Putnam, an **imprint** of Penguin Random House. But Marisa did have a small and thriving newsletter and a few media hits under her belt.

Most important, she had a great big idea—she contextualized attachment theory through the lens of friendship. Attachment theory, a psychological approach often used in therapy, usually explains romantic or parent-child relationships, but it's not commonly seen as useful to platonic relationships. Universal theme (friendship), meet unique angle (attachment theory). Marisa also had what every agent and editor is looking for in an author partner: the determination to be the go-to person in their field. *Platonic* became a *New York Times* bestseller in its first week because Marisa's unique angle easily grabbed the attention of many readers interested in the topic of friendship.

First let's identify your book's universal theme. Search your favorite online retailer for books that are similar to yours. When you read their descriptions, what are the key words that keep coming up? What qualities do these similar books have? Are there descriptive words or phrases you see over and over, such as "a story of love and loss" or "a humorous coming-of-age novel"? This can be a good starting place for determining the universal theme of your book.

If your novel is an 18th-century romance, your universal theme might be the dynamics between women and men throughout history. Or it could be related to a lesson or teaching, such as building relationships or unlearning toxic habits. Maybe there's a great David and Goliath story to be written from out of your detective novel or narrative nonfiction, but you have been focusing on the obvious character. It's the character you overlooked who is wrestling with feelings of inadequacy, desperate to prove himself, universalizing the underdog in all of us.

Pick up a book from your reading pile. When you flip it over to read the description, you should see at least one theme mentioned in the last paragraph of the synopsis.

Now, what differentiates your book from these titles? Do you have a different perspective on these themes or a personal experience that adds something else? Is there a fight you want to pick with commonly heard advice? If you can't think of anything that separates your book from those you admire, you need to rework your idea.

The Timely/Timeless Equation

Now that you've identified your universal theme and unique point of view, let's explore how your book meets the second parameter for a big idea of being both timely *and* timeless.

A book is timely when it fits within a larger cultural conversation, specifically one that has been given attention by the media. It answers the question all agents and editors ask every time they receive a pitch: Why is this book important right now? Have there been regular news stories or social media chatter relevant to your subject? Is there a prominent television series connected to your work that has everyone talking?

In the industry, we refer to timely books that are destined to capture media interest as having *frontlist* appeal. This basically means that because your book concept is zeitgeisty and fresh, it should sell well in the short term, gaining momentum right out of the gate.

Publishers wish to see timeliness because it poises you for national news attention, where a wide audience will learn about your book through television, radio, print, online features, podcasts, or social media. For Paul Whitlatch, executive editor at Crown, an imprint of Penguin Random House, "It's always the dream that a book is not just responding to events, but that the book is so good, it can actually drive the story and create revelations." Agents need to think like book editors, and editors need to think like the media.

What do these parties have in common? A vested interest in the reader.

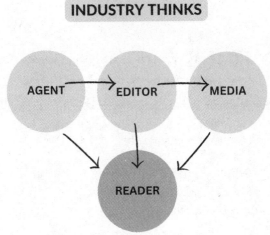

HOW THE INDUSTRY THINKS

AGENT → EDITOR → MEDIA

READER

Two of Jodi Picoult's novels, *Nineteen Minutes* and *The Pact*, address the heartbreaking but topical circumstances in the United States of a school shooting and a teen suicide. Similarly, the book *We Need to Talk About Kevin*, by Lionel Shriver, hit such a nerve about teen violence, it was soon adapted into a movie. Book review coverage has been diminishing for years, and arguably novelists have been the most sorely affected. When you touch on a hot-button issue, authors can find their work exponentially amplified by the media.

Even better: when one book benefits from press attention, it points to how a future book can benefit too. Matthew Walker's *New York Times* bestseller *Why We Sleep* gave the topic of sleep a moment in mainstream culture. Capitalizing on the hot topic, Ada Calhoun published *Why We Can't Sleep: Women's New Midlife Crisis*. As her perfect title suggests, she discusses the common condition of insomnia but from the uncommon angle of midlife women and their specific burdens. She smartly gave the media (and readers) a new way to talk about a topic of fascination and consequence.

TRY IT: IS YOUR BOOK TIMELY?

A few soft data points can be used to measure a book's timeliness. Answer these questions to see what could be timely about your idea:

- What are those around you talking about?
- Is there a trend in those conversations that your book can capture?
- What's the point of contention?
- What are the books in your genre that everyone is avidly discussing?

Any combination of these data points will lead you toward the timeliness factor for your book.

18

But that's not all. You still need to think critically about how your book could be considered time*less*. A timeless book is a long-term earner. While the industry is appetized by media attention, we're not looking for a flash in the pan success. If your idea does not have the enduring value to carry it beyond the transience of media or a reader's short attention span, it usually won't be a book publishers will value seriously. Even more critical than frontlist appeal is what's called **backlist** appeal. The book that "backlists" can sell several years following its publication or even many years after that.

Delia Owens's *Where the Crawdads Sing* provides a model example of this perennial quality. It blends a coming-of-age story and ode to the natural world through a young girl who finds friends in the seagulls and peace in the sands that she can't find in proper society. As a very different example, in the searingly dystopian *The Handmaid's Tale*, Margaret Atwood describes a future where a woman's freedom is taken from her and she has to find the will to survive. These themes that explore the human condition—female independence, opportunity, and societal roles—will be germane for years to come.

The Body Keeps the Score is one of my favorite examples of striking the perfect balance between timely and timeless. Eight years after it was originally published, it became a household name and held a #1 spot on the *New York Times* bestseller list for over 200 consecutive weeks.[1] Its massive spike in popularity occurred around the onset of a global pandemic that sparked people's curiosity about how the brain and the body influence each other. At that moment, mental health was in crisis, trauma was the word of the day, and with a sudden increase in time spent alone indoors, people began reevaluating their relationships with themselves. The author took a timely approach to health, a timeless topic.

TRY IT: IS YOUR BOOK TIMELESS?

Here are a few questions to evaluate the timelessness of your book idea.

- Have you incorporated universal themes?
- Are there similar books to yours, published years ago but still being discussed?
- Does your book have the capacity to make a difference in people's lives?
- Could someone buy this book years down the line and still be able to apply it to their life?

Striking the Balance Between Timely/Timeless

Imagine we were at a writer's conference together and you were speed pitching me. How would your book capture both the timely and the timeless? Below are two demonstrations of what this might sound like to practice out loud.

PITCH #1: A nonfiction book on how to solve burnout and fatigue and restore cognitive function.

MY TAKE: There's a vast and urgent problem you're solving, which is a selling point. But what distinguishes it from so many burnout books out there?

THE REFRAME: Argue that the core problem with our energy levels lies within our cells, particularly with the mitochondria. Spotlighting this little-known term in the book's pitch makes it timely and intriguing while maintaining scientific integrity.

PITCH #2: A work of fiction about a woman whose fiancé dies young. Depressed, she thinks her life is over, until she somehow finds a way to enter a world where he is still alive but everything is different. She bounces between two worlds, but no one believes that she possesses supernatural powers, and she can't decide which world she wants.

MY TAKE: What is the main character's struggle? Why doesn't she just stay in the world with her fiancé?

THE REFRAME: A novel about a young woman whose fiancé dies in a car accident and she finds a "doorway" through which she can live two lives: one where his death didn't occur and she is with him, and one where he does die, and she has to live on without him. The main character toils between these two lives, struggling to decide which life she wants and considering a new person who wants her to stay.

One of my favorite stories to tell writers is the story of my client Susan Peirce Thompson. Susan, the author of two *New York Times* best-selling books, *Bright Line Eating* and *The Official Bright Line Eating Cookbook*, began much like you did, with just the whisper of an idea. Susan had me transfixed at first pitch. She was a former drug addict who, against all odds, became a neuroscientist, only to realize her coping mechanisms came from never having felt comfortable with her own body. Inspired by her own struggles, she began studying the issue. When she discovered the science behind food addiction, she found that this was the toughest addiction to kick.

We discussed the possibilities of a memoir, but something was telling us both that this idea was smaller than it had the potential to be. A compelling personal story has its place in any self-help book. It's vital that our teachers practice what they preach so we can relate to them as human beings who are just like us—flawed and aspiring to be something better. But in a best-case scenario, the teaching extends far beyond the teacher.

At the time of our first conversation, Susan had a small but successful business, where she was onto something interesting: a game-changing, science-based approach for thinking about weight loss with a genuine empathy for "food addiction" that was not limited to the obese or those struggling with eating disorders. This wasn't your typical diet book, and I recognized that immediately. Whether physical or psychological, Susan had tapped into a timeless nerve—wellness. And given the current obesity crisis in America, there was an urgency to address the issue immediately. Susan had also developed the great hook of a self-assessment tool and diet for those who struggled with food addiction to finally find the "right-sized bodies" they longed for.

Now this was a great package—one that I could not take the chance of missing. Susan's "why" was to help the thousands of people worldwide who struggled with food and weight gain and to fight the larger global obesity crisis. Her angle (unique point of view) was to do it through the neuroscience of food addiction.

TRY IT: DISCOVER YOUR BIG IDEA

Discovering your big idea is something that will take time and effort. To help you, here are some guidelines with an exercise to put it all together.

1. Determine your area of passion and expertise.

Let your natural curiosity lead you to the area you will explore for readers, whether you're writing about parenting, sports, science, young adult romance, a family history, or the future—really, any topic that would excite you to talk about not for months but for years to come. Let's say you are a sociology professor who is passionate about discussing diversity's role in the world of parenting. Your big idea almost certainly exists within your realm of expertise.

2. Figure out what's popular in your space.

Following in the vein of the parenting book example, look up what the most popular parenting books are right now or in the last three years. You might notice many of the books include mindfulness and emotion-focused discipline techniques or new terminologies like "gentle parenting" or "paleo parenting." Parents will always want to get better at parenting—that is universal. In recent years, they have often looked to accomplish this by understanding their child and the latest research. How can you build on that conversation within your topic?

For another example, let's look at romance novels, which are selling better than ever, pointing to a global craving readers are experiencing to escape from their own lives. The more exotic and adventurous the better, as people want to imagine themselves anywhere but in the confines of their homes. This rudimentary understanding of your genre can guide you toward creating something commercial.

3. Pinpoint what you uniquely add to the conversation.

If there are countless books about parenting in the modern world, but no one has yet written about it through the academic lens of research on diversity, then you've found a possible hook. If you're writing a novel, maybe your idea is a zombie or vampire character who has an interesting trait, like a love for animals and an ability to communicate with them.

4. Ensure that your big idea requires a written book in the first place.

This last step has become a major challenge in recent years: if your idea already exists as free web, video, speech, or podcast content, there needs to be something contained in your pages worth a price that cannot be mimicked online. You might follow Steps 1–3 perfectly, but if your book idea can be covered in an essay or podcast episode, you still haven't landed the plane, and agents and editors are likely to reject your work. Your big idea should have a simple headline promise but with more detail and nuance to unravel. There needs to be meat on the bones, as we say.

The biggest ideas are out there. You just need to grab them and package them in a compelling and relevant way. Allow yourself room for inspiration and creativity, but let this flow hand in hand with your research. In today's market, saturated with content of every kind, I see too many writers make the mistake of dusting an old book off the shelf, or locking themselves away in the proverbial ivory tower, then simply sending their work out into the world. The more investigating you do, the clearer you will be about the unique value of your work. How to do that, exactly, will become more evident to you in the chapter ahead.

STEP 2

Decide Your Differentiator

Dear Lucinda,
I'm confused if I need to include comparative titles in
my pitch. And do I have to commit to a single genre if
my novel is a mystery, thriller, and romance?

— LISA (WENTZVILLE, MO)

After you have your big idea, it's time to decide where your book fits into the publishing landscape and what sets it apart from existing titles. I call this your differentiator, and it's one of the most valuable things any first-time writer can bring to the table. To discover this, all you'll need is a little tool called Amazon. (At the time of writing this book, traditional publishers still sell 60 to 70 percent of their books via this online giant.[2])

This step is about how to use Amazon or your online bookseller of choice to show agents that there is demand for your book and confidently explain why. It's time to become a book detective.

I'm a sucker for books that are science-backed and reveal a surprising twist. When Jonathan, a Canadian Ph.D., blindly submitted his query, our intern snatched it up right away. "The title doesn't work," she reported matter-of-factly. "But he's a fit for our *list*; he has credentials, an impressive online platform for an academic, and it's a fresh topic."

Jonathan had more than done his research. He had watched every single one of our videos and had read our company blog assiduously. Looking closely at **Publishers Marketplace**, he could tell that the publishers we did business with were the right candidates for his project. And on a personal level, Jonathan noted that I had attended McGill and represented a number of Canadian authors.

What Jonathan did not know was that I was looking for the next big book on misinformation. His unique angle was an exploration of pseudoscience—how so many members of society came to trust it and how to use science literacy to discern the grifters from the healers. When agents and editors consider books, we look for ones that will enlighten us or the people we know. We think about these people quite concretely—a best friend, an aunt, a father-in-law, a spouse—who would come to the book eagerly or be served by it in some way. At that serendipitous moment Jonathan's query arrived, several of my friends suffering from afflictions they could not understand were falling into the expensive trap of questionable wellness practices. They needed this book to get informed and get well.

The second reason I was drawn to Jonathan's idea had more to do with its commercial viability. I had taken notice of his **comparative titles**, or "comps," books published in the last few years with a similar audience. In Jonathan's case, they were similar books that addressed the topic of misinformation: Tim Caulfield's *Relax, Dammit* and Dr. Jen

Gunter's *The Vagina Bible*. By including them, Jonathan tipped the scale in his favor. The best comps have many positive reviews and have sold tens of thousands of copies. Comps get agents excited when they are called to imagine the bestseller that your book could be, which is exactly what happened when I read Jonathan's pitch.

To this day, I think that the reason Jonathan's impressive talent was overlooked by other agencies was due to a title and tone that missed the mark at first blush. But fortunately, we saw incredible potential in that query letter—in the idea, in the writing, in the industriousness and confidence of the author, and perhaps most important, in its market appeal. The use of two perfect comp titles immediately gave me a vision for what this book could be.

It's entirely natural that as a creative with something original to say, you may find it difficult to choose the right comps. You worry that a particular book is too fluffy for your taste, that the author has a mixed reputation, or that the writer is just so extraordinary that your book couldn't possibly sit beside theirs. But when you approach agents with your pitch, it is critical to show confidence in your knowledge. No matter who you are or what you're writing, the capacity for knowledge is a skill that every one of you can hone. This is why comps are a querier's secret weapon. If you have nothing but comps to appeal to an agent, you're closer than you think to landing your pitch.

IS YOUR GENRE RIGHT?

You will come to use comps in many ways and, most critically to this process, in your query letter. But to choose the right comps, let's make sure that you have identified the best genre for your book first. How certain are you that you are writing narrative nonfiction versus a memoir? Or a literary novel versus commercial fiction? There are nuances to genre, and picking one almost always means making a sacrifice of some kind; parting with what you envisaged your book to be in favor of what it actually is. In my coaching practice, I've found that nearly every writer starting out ends up reconceiving their genre by the end of our work together. Even my more seasoned clients have discovered the power of making a switch, and the wider readership they never imagined could be theirs as a result.

While it sounds obvious, many people neglect this detail in their pitches—they believe their book straddles three genres, or they are simply afraid to commit to one. They haven't done their research on comparative titles that can provide vital clues. As a result, they omit genre from their pitch entirely, leaving an overly subscribed agent or publisher to figure it out for them.

Whether you are making a pitch to an agent or a reader, the best thing you can do is tempt the imagination but eliminate guesswork. Publishers need an easy "get," which begins with how to categorize a book to booksellers. Remembering this should help you in any part of the process. If you haven't labeled your book's genre, there's a good chance you've already lost our attention.

So many writers ask, "But what if I choose wrong? Will I blow my chances of getting an agent?" Not at all. Here's a piece of advice that might surprise you. When you are unsure about genre, take your best guess. It's just like the SAT: you can afford to get the answer wrong, but you can't afford to leave it blank. While your agent and publishing partners may take a different or more expansive view of categorizing your book later, you must first convince them there is a clear genre for your book in the first place. It's not as important that you be right as it is that you make a good case.

Years ago, I snatched up a query from my slush pile by a sought-after speaker who teaches evolutionary biology to executives. Her book's argument was that our ancestral selves give us blind spots in how we manage people. She categorized it as a business book, but based on her fresh and counterintuitive idea, I immediately knew it could reach a wider audience—and command a larger advance—as a self-improvement book. She had given her best shot at categorizing her book, and even if it wasn't quite right yet, I still reached out to her.

Familiarizing yourself with genre works very much the same way as writing Amazon descriptions. Identifying the key components of your book and searching for books that feature the same components as your big idea is key. Let me share a way to do just that.

Go to Amazon, click on the first book you find, and scroll all the way down to Product Details. Next, check for your chosen title's Best Seller Rank. Amazon organizes its bestsellers by genre. A title like *The Secret History* by Donna Tartt is a top seller in psychological thrillers, literary fiction, and suspense thrillers. If your book has similar components to *The Secret History*, then it should have elements of the thriller genre and will market well to that readership.

Likewise, James Clear's *Atomic Habits* was a massive bestseller in the categories of business, social psychology, and self-help. If you are writing a book about habits, you might want to consider attaching your book to these genres. You'll notice that these books rank and are categorized in multiple genres. For the purposes of your pitch, just settle on the one that best reflects your book. And my advice from above applies again: if you are unsure, make your best guess.

Here is a comprehensive list of genres from which to choose.*

GENRES
The Ultimate List

ADULT

FICTION:
Debut,
Commercial, Literary,
Horror, Inspirational,
Mystery/Crime,
New Adult, Paranormal,
Sci-Fi/Fantasy,
Thriller, Romance,
General/Other

NONFICTION:
Self-help, Anthology,
Biography, Body/Mind/Spirit,
Business/Finance, Pop Culture,
Diet, Food/Beverage, Health/
Medicine, History, How-to,
Humor, Illustrated/Art, Memoir,
Narrative, Parenting, Politics,
Religion/Spirituality, Science/
Tech, Sports, True Crime

CHILDREN'S

Fantasy, Graphic Novel,
Middle Grade Fiction,
Middle Grade Nonfiction,
Picture Book Fiction,
Picture Book Nonfiction,
Young Adult

Agents need to understand genre in order to conceptualize your book in the current market and to visualize how they will sell it to editors. You would be amazed by how many so-called inspirational guides to health and wellness will be seen as pure memoir, or that the "big idea" book you thought would establish you as a thought leader is just a niche business book for those who work in your field. It's okay to get it wrong, but let's get you as close to the right genre as we can. Here are just a few miscategorized books we see time and time again.

---

* *According to Publishers Marketplace, 2023*

The memoir disguised as a business book.

Business books generally educate or solve a problem. Your personal story may appeal to the readership, and many of the best business books are quite personal. But if most of your business book is just your own story and opinions without any exploration of why or how things work, you have not identified the big idea discussed in Step 1. A memoir by an entrepreneur or CEO is generally seen as sellable only when your company is a household name.

The memoir posing as personal growth.

Memoir is one of the easiest genres to mischaracterize because so many nonfiction books do contain much of the author's own experiences. But there is much more to a memoir than that. If most of your book is prescriptive or how-to based on something you have learned, it would be better to say that you're writing a personal growth title.

The science fiction fantasy (or any) novel billed as young adult.

Just because the main character of your novel is a younger person doesn't mean that your book has the contemporary vernacular or ethos that would speak to the average teenager!

The mystery pitched as a thriller.

The difference here can seem subtle, as are many differences in the fiction genres, but it is important to understand. The best way to distinguish between a thriller and a mystery is to look at the core narrative of your story. Is your main character actually piecing together clues? Then it is a mystery. Or is most of the content focused on suspense, dread, and the fear of the future? Then it is a thriller. Unsure? Call it a mystery thriller. Pro tip: your book will be seen as more marketable if it contains the fast-paced, engrossing qualities of a thriller.

TRY IT: DETERMINE YOUR BOOK'S GENRE

1. Search online booksellers, retail stores, and best-seller lists for the genre that you believe is right for your book. When you leaf through the first five or so titles listed, do you see any of the following elements that are similar to yours?

theme	writing
topic	style
character traits	intended audience
setting	patterns
stories	exercises or images
structure	

2. Make a list of these similarities.

3. If you don't notice any, try the next genre.

4. Choose the genre you feel is most fitting, and don't sweat it. These can always be changed or customized to the agent or publisher receiving your pitch.

And just like that, you have a solid, research-backed foundation to support you in classifying your book's genre, which should lend you confidence. Agents will instantly recognize the tropes they've seen before at a glance. You've made it a clear "get."

And if your research leads you to pivot from the genre you had originally conceived, do not resist. Your genre will be decided upon collaboratively with your agent. Editors too may later lend their opinions. It's a process that will evolve with time.

USE COMPS TO SIGNIFICANTLY INCREASE YOUR BOOK'S POTENTIAL

Agents and editors want to see your creation "in conversation" with other books out there. Putting in comps does not make your project sound unoriginal; on the contrary, comps strengthen your query by giving the reader a better sense of what to expect from your story and make them excited to see your spin on it. Your main goal in researching and using comp titles in a query is to prove to agents that your book will be popular. Here is a brief list of the ways you will use comp titles in your publishing journey:

1. In your query letter to help describe and animate your idea to agents.

2. In your elevator pitch when quickly explaining your book in interviews and to readers.

3. To compensate for a weakness in your pitch, like a lack of platform or name recognition.

Like Hollywood, publishing is a lookalike business. If your book looks like a few titles that have proven to be popular, your chances of making an argument for your book's potential, especially as a first-time author, drastically increase when you call them to a person's mind.

When querying, agents want you to be specific as to why those books are comparative so we can get a quick mental snapshot of what your book looks like. Does your book have the tenderness of *Aristotle and Dante Discover the Secrets of the Universe* melded with the immersive world-building of *Howl's Moving Castle*? What about each title does your book carry over, and how does your book offer a unique spin? Go for two to three specific comps that match your book, ideally with at least one in the same genre.

35

Don't go for *Harry Potter* if you are writing something like an adult historical fiction novel or memoir. Books that are not anywhere in the realm of the same genre will not persuade anyone of your book's commercial appeal, nor does using them express the research you have done or the realism of your expectations. If you can demonstrate your market knowledge and realistic expectations for your book, you will strike the perfect balance.

Another reason comps are important: behind the scenes, editors will often draft what's called a *profit and loss*, or P&L, statement based on your comps to project sales. Using just a couple of well-performing titles can help make the case for an acquisition.

In nonfiction book proposals, you get the chance to expand on your comp titles and make an even stronger case for your book's potential. There, you can describe five or so titles and go into more detail about the similarities and differences they share. For the purposes of your pitch, though, just focus on a few comps that share the most similar characteristics with your book and/or describe a unique aspect of it. Feel free to get us excited with contemporary blockbusters, or what we call "category crushers," books that dominate the whole category (think *The Vanishing Half* or *Start with Why*).

Comps have to be a good fit, not a perfect fit, so I encourage you to lose the perfectionism that is natural to you as a writer but isn't always useful when it comes time to pitch. Comps don't even have to be books! Although at least one should be, I love to use comps like films, TV shows, popular music albums, or even video games in my pitches to editors. Agents and editors are well versed across media formats. They are trend-casters and futurists, consuming much of what is currently popular and relevant. If you are writing a novel about zombies, maybe the television show and video game *The Last of Us* gives recipients the best snapshot rather than an older success like *World War Z*. Or perhaps your YA novel about teenagers in love has the swoony vibes of Taylor Swift's *Folklore* album.

If your book is "something meets something," that fusion can be especially intriguing and potentially define your book's appeal better than you could yourself. The "X meets Y" equation does the hard work for you, and this is how agents, editors, and producers speak to one another all the time. Think of it in terms of "like but different." An even more sophisticated approach is to use comps to explain how your book is similar to one style of book but intended for a different audience or written with particular characteristics ("with the suspense of X, the lyrical writing of Y, and the timeless appeal of Z"). My most successful pitches to editors create this patchwork effect.

To give context, below are some examples and templates for how your comps might feature in your query letter. Several of these examples are books by authors my agency works with and the exact wording we used in our own pitch letters to editors. Once you get the hang of using these analogies, you may just begin to speak in comps in your everyday life—making any concept accessible to your listener.

Here's what I mean:

Fiction: "A mix between *The Time Traveler's Wife* and *Outlander*, my book . . ." or "*The Hitchhiker's Guide to the Galaxy* for kids . . ."

Memoir: "Part memoir, part survival guide, and a cross between *Educated* and *Miracle Country*, my book weaves stories of growing up in a cult with lessons from nature."

Nonfiction/Self-Help: "Experts like Peter Walsh and even Julie Morgenstern have been penning bestsellers about tidying for decades. Marie Kondo, whose books include the #1 *New York Times* bestseller *The Life-Changing*

Magic of Tidying Up and *Spark Joy*, is the latest bona fide craze. I believe I have a unique perspective and patented method that can make my book a tidying classic."

Children's: "My book will be a clean version of the popular title *Go the F**k to Sleep*. Parents who want a charming, funny, rhyming picture book about getting your child to sleep without the swearing will find it here."

CREATE YOUR OWN AMAZON DESCRIPTION

Once you find a comp that has similar themes, tropes, or messages as your own work, study the description that is available on Amazon. In most cases, the top minds in marketing at publishing houses created those descriptions, and you can mimic their craft. How can you reverse-engineer them to your advantage?

Take this Amazon description for a novel surrounding a family saga:

> *Twenty-six-year-old Maia has never had a child, but she is a mother—of six siblings and cousins who have no one else.* **[Intrigue/setup]** *The Lopez family used to be a force of nature, a wealthy and tight-knit clan who essentially ran the small town of Burgess, South Carolina. But last year, everything changed, and they were plunged into poverty and estrangement.* **[Drama]**
>
> *Now, Maia is trying her best to keep her generation of Lopezes together, while still trying to reckon with the fall. Complicating this mission is the strange and threatening letters she keeps receiving about the past and future of the Lopez family.* **[High stakes]** *How did they get here? And, more pressingly, how will they survive?* **[Suspense]**

This description is designed to hook you. Notice its structure: in the first paragraph, it establishes the five *W's*—the who, what, where, when, why of it all; our main character; and the setting through which the story progresses. Next, the description introduces the stakes for our main character: survival. What do your characters stand to lose? What is the thing that your heroine would never dream of doing, that by the end of your novel, she is forced to do? What makes the narrative propulsive, a characteristic editors always look for?

THE 5 W'S

Writing Your Book's Description?
Answer the 5 W's

WHO?
Briefly describe your main characters
Establish your protagonist, antagonist, and key players.

WHAT?
Set up the plot
What's happening in your story and where will it lead?

WHERE?
Name your setting
Let readers know where your story will take place.

WHEN?
Establish time period
Is the story contemporary? Or does it take place in the future? The past?

WHY?
The driving force
What is your protagonist's goal?

If the five *W*'s sound familiar, it's because you were probably taught them in a writing class or in a book about craft. The description you create should mimic this approach, cluing us in to the highlights of what actually happens in your book rather than focusing solely on the attributes or emotions of your characters, a mistake I see so many first-time writers make in their query letters. Instead, your query letter should follow this plot-forward approach.

You can equally detect at least four of the *W*'s in a description for a personal development title. The formula for a self-help Amazon description is often in the vein of the following:

> *In this all-you-need guide to living your best life, productivity expert _____* [who] *cuts through the noise to show you how to reach your goals* [what]—*and stick to them. Every January, we write up a list of things we want to do; inevitably, by February, we're the same old people we've always been* [when]. *What are we doing wrong?*
>
> *With an enjoyable balance of academic research and personable humor, _____ will teach you why goal-setting is so tricky* [why], *and more important, he'll tell you the six simple ways to make it easier.*

For nonfiction, "who" is the author/expert, "why" and "when" both relate to the timeliness factor of the book, and "what" is the topic or solution offered in its pages. You'll notice there is no "where" like there is for fiction, as setting is obviously not necessary in many nonfiction books, though it would be for narrative genres like memoir.

Practicing how you would write your own Amazon description further helps you decide and communicate how your book is different from others out there. And there is no reason to reinvent the wheel here. Study how comps are rendered to dissect how they're being distinguished from the rest of the market.

Go Further Down the Rabbit Hole

If you're inclined to excavate more deeply, look at the "Products Related to This Item" or "What Do Customers Buy After Viewing This Item" Amazon lists to use as comps. For example, suggested titles to buy for fans of the mega-popular *Dune* series include *The Atlas Six* and the *Game of Thrones* series. But while these big titles are often marketed as the standard, the smaller titles are where I want to draw your focus next.

By doing research into the descriptions of titles that are not as well known, you can see how they allude to big bestsellers to supplement the strength of their own narratives and hook an audience. A deeper dive into the Amazon search engine leads you to another science-fiction series called Starship's Mage with a respectable 2,000+ reviews. If you are writing a *Dune*-like book, this might be a more realistic comp to suggest than *Dune* or its huge contemporaries.

Study the Amazon descriptions of the comparative books in your genre and use those to find more. Leave no stone unturned, and you will become better and better at distilling and communicating your idea to others.

TRY IT:
USE AMAZON
TO YOUR ADVANTAGE

1. Find a Book Like Yours

Once you find a comp that has similar themes, tropes, or messages as your own work, try studying the description that is available on Amazon.

2. Use Amazon's Suggested Titles

Look for the suggested titles at the bottom of this book's Amazon page. In the smaller books' descriptions, you can see how they use the bigger books to supplement the strength of their own narratives and hook their audience.

3. Find Realistic Comps

Look to Amazon's numbers to find realistic yet successful comps, with a decent amount of reviews and a solid rating. The bestsellers are great for describing your book, but a lesser-known comp shows you are well read and understand your genre.

4. Practice Writing Your Own Synopsis

Synthesize your favorite descriptions: which books made you want to "Add to Cart"? Use these effective descriptions as inspiration for writing your query letter's synopsis and include the best fits as comps in your letter.

USE COMPS TO REVIVE THE TIMELESS CLASSIC

But my comp is fifty years old. Will it age me? In terms of making your book relevant today, it's important to choose books that have been published in the last five or even two years. If you are itching to reference older master-pieces very much in need of an update, you need to clearly describe your book's new take and show us why it's the perfect time to publish it. My aforementioned client Dan Martell said in his pitch that *Buy Back Your Time* would be a new version of *The E-Myth*, a business book staple origi-nally published in 1986.

For more recent publications, look again at their Amazon pages: Has the book hit a bestseller list or won an award? What is the volume and quality of reviews? I con-sider 100 or more reviews as a good indication of a book that has performed (sold) well.

The publishers behind the similar titles you find are another critical consideration. If you're looking for a major publisher, but you select books from lesser-known small presses, you will give the impression that your book is niche—possibly too niche for a major publisher to consider. Since you are aiming to get signed by an agent, do not choose comps that are self- or **hybrid-published**. As successful as those books might have been, agents want to see books that were published by a **trade press**. These are books that are given larger dis-tribution and thus possess the potential for far higher advances and wider commercial success.

POSITIONING YOUR BOOK

Once you have selected comps and reverse-engineered ex-actly how an Amazon description has hooked you, you have learned the art of positioning—and you can apply it to your own work. Positioning simply means how your book sits in the marketplace compared to other books, and it's a term agents and editors take seriously. If we can't figure out the positioning of your book, we will not acquire it. But since your book can't just win a popularity contest or resemble other models of success, you also need that unique angle we discussed in Step 1. I'll emphasize this again because it's so important. You need to be different. This is how you prove to agents that not only will your book be popular, but it will also be new—the winning combination we look for.

TRY IT: THE POSITIONING EQUATION

Now you know that your comps have to be recent, relevant, and popular. The differentiator is what is unique to your book that other titles failed to deliver or haven't yet explored. To help you properly position your book, I've come up with a little equation:

Comps + Differentiator = Book with Promise

COMPS

DIFFERENTIATOR

This isn't always easy, so here is a list of questions to help you determine your differentiator:

For fiction:

- What makes your plot rare?

- What's the most surprising twist to your plot?

- What are some characteristics, shown through either narrative, themes, or characters, that distinguish your book from others like it?

For nonfiction:

- What's the most surprising thing you've learned in your area of exploration that you wish to share with others?

- What makes your perspective unique?

- Why are you a new voice that readers should listen to?

- What message will readers take away that they haven't heard before?

Your differentiator ups the ante from a generic book that doesn't sell to a book that publishers will line up to buy at auction. I've seen it happen!

In interviews for his book launch, my client Ron Friedman immediately hooked listeners and readers with this pitch: "We've all been taught that there are two paths to greatness: practice and talent. But it turns out that there is a third path that many don't know about. It's called reverse-engineering, and it's what my book *Decoding Greatness* is all about." Did you catch the surprise element? We all think there are two ways, but there is actually a third.

For *Gone Girl*, it would sound more like this: "Amy goes missing, and her husband is suspected of murder. But the sweet, diary-writing Amy of the first half of the book is revealed to be a very different woman in the second half of the novel." Not only do we now know that a shocking twist is in store for us, but we're also told just enough that we're left wanting more.

ACE YOUR TITLE

Many of the best writers know how to hook their audience from their very first interaction: the title of their book. Dr. Benjamin Hardy, psychologist and personal development author of *Be Your Future Self Now* and *Personality Isn't Permanent*, told me, "Title really does matter. How you frame the book matters." Love them or hate them, a title should immediately intrigue or make a statement.

Whether the title changes later, it's the most straightforward way to get an agent's instant attention. And titles that challenge the status quo and seem controversial at first glance have been known to be effective sellers time and again. Take Mark Manson's *The Subtle Art of Not Giving a F*ck* and Jennette McCurdy's memoir *I'm Glad My Mom Died*, for example. Jayne Allen's *Black Girls Must Die Exhausted* stopped me dead in my tracks. I had to pick up the manuscript just on the basis of its title.

When you research comps, it's a great time to begin workshopping your own book title and subtitle and work backward to analyze why certain book titles stand out. Take a look at Ben Hardy's titles again. The immediacy of the promise in *Be Your Future Self Now* and frankness of *Personality Isn't Permanent* are arresting. It leaves a reader no room for ambiguity. Conversely, instead of giving it all away up front, a title that intrigues like Laura Dave's *The Last Thing He Told Me* is equally compelling. "What was the last thing he told you?!" readers want to know. Title will be the last *T* to cross to ensure a compelling pitch when you write your query letter. Ideally, your title will capture the big-idea elements we covered in Step 1.

Titles are often determined right down to the wire, so again, please don't worry about making it perfect. The likelihood is that it won't be! But my general guideline is this: be as big and bold as possible. Don't be afraid to be a bit controversial or to make someone uncomfortable. Your title can (and often should) be a hook in of itself.

Try this fun and productive activity the next time you meet with your writers' group or even at the next social gathering you're hosting. Create what Ann Patchett calls a "title wall." Jot down the titles you're considering on Post-Its and hang them on a bulletin board or write them on index cards and place them on a table. Have the group remove the Post-its or cards they don't like. Their reasoning for what they have removed and what they've kept may offer a breakthrough. They may also have better suggestions! The best titles are road tested.

With your newfound grasp of positioning, stellar comps, and your very best effort at a book title, you've already achieved three big wins for creating a book with potential.

Now it's time to find your readers.

STEP 3

Pinpoint What
Your Reader Craves

Dear Lucinda,
I've been asked a few times now, "Who is your book
for?" I want to say, "Everyone!" but that feels like a
wrong answer. How do I answer this question?

— AMY (GREENVILLE, SC)

"A book for everyone is a book for no one." When I heard that line early in my career, it was an "aha!" moment for me. Like so many writers, I had always thought that the more people your book claims to reach, the better! But the truth is that most books start narrow, with a distinct set of readers.

In the following pages, you'll discover why people buy books, how to identify your readers, and the three ways your book can appeal to them. Defining your readership is about much more than age and gender, although those are important demographics. Instead, it's about being clear on the purpose your book delivers.

FOCUS ON TRANSFORMATION

The best way to understand your reader is to begin by asking: What are readers looking for? Most books are centered around the promise of a transformation. Novels focus on how their characters grow and evolve, though one could argue that the most excellent fiction transforms its characters and readers alike. Universally, I believe readers come to a book for at least one of three reasons:

1. It solves a problem.

2. It delves deep into a fascinating subject.

3. It provides entertainment and delight.

Let's dive into what all this means.

Solve a Problem

What top editors have impressed upon me time and again is that for categories like personal development, health, inspirational, and other expertise-driven books, your big idea must address a pain point that readers have and propose a radical solution they haven't seen before. For example, let's say you're an expert in environmental science and you notice people in the communities where you perform research are having problems with the drinking water quality, leading to a higher rate of disease and mortality.

You do more digging and realize there are thousands of communities suffering from a similar problem but very little media coverage about it and no legislative efforts to address it. You have your problem. Now you need to expose this issue to the benefit of the people who are impacted so that readers learn of their problems and get involved.

Often your readers are already aware of a pressing challenge they have and are actively searching for a solution that online fodder or podcasts cannot solve for them decisively. They know they need to take a first step toward improving their circumstances and are willing to spend the price tag of a book for information and guidance that could be life-changing. This was the case for the readers of *Cashing Out*, a personal finance book by my clients Julien and Kiersten Saunders. They knew that Black Americans were fed up with the advice to work hard, make money, save, and invest—advice that appeared far easier for a more advantaged white population. Formerly in corporate roles themselves, Julien and Kiersten brought a personal viewpoint. The couple wrote *Cashing Out* to teach readers how to achieve financial security, quit high-stress jobs, and retake control of their finances. Their mission was to create more Black millionaires than the world had ever seen. Because they had worked with (and been) underappreciated and underpaid Black Americans for many years, they understood this was a tangible pain point for their reader.

Pain Points for Self-Improvement Writers

Sometimes I have to talk clients into seeing themselves as "self-help" writers. Many writers' first instinct is often to tell their life story as memoir. But not only is memoir arguably the most competitive category, a memoir often won't deliver the greatest value or reach as wide a readership if you aren't a known name. You may bristle at the label, but self-help, otherwise known as self-improvement or personal growth titles, sales are skyrocketing. So many of you have valuable lessons to share. So who's to say a useful book can't also be a work of art? That philosophy is old news. And if you are largely unknown as a writer or on social media, the unique experience and the fresh insights you offer can compensate for a smaller platform.

If you really want to make an impact, you might follow the lead of our student-turned-client Sara McElroy. Initially, her idea was to write a collection of essays about women in the workforce experiencing burnout, especially as it had been exacerbated by the pandemic. Later, she considered memoir. While her tack had a great relatable element (who wasn't burned out by the pandemic?), it was still centrally focused on her own journey. Sara and I had multiple discussions figuring out what the angle should be, and ultimately *Women Who Walk* became a narrative self-help guide that gives women the confidence and tools to leave jobs that no longer serve them. Sara didn't have to remove the personal elements, but she was able to expand her idea to lean in to her journalistic interests and create something that would help many women and truly have an impact.

Many nonfiction books, and especially self-help books, boil down to only three categories that are proven, in my experience, to have profound need and urgency. They are:

1. Health

2. Wealth

3. Relationships

Health and wealth are obvious categories. If someone is suffering from burnout, they may be looking for literature on the best practices to try. If someone is struggling to save money, a book that promises long-lasting wealth cuts right to the heart of their worry. Stronger relationships make us feel more connected at work and at home.

What I believe unites these categories, what every self-help reader looks for, is freedom. That big-ticket promise— to liberate us from sadness, to elevate us, to untether us from pain—is the transformation from where we are to where we want to be. What I've also discovered about the psychology of book readers is that all of us are, on some level, profoundly lonely. We are looking for our challenges to be seen, our perspective to be heard, or to be touched on some level that we cannot internally provide for ourselves.

Here are some expressions of readers' pain points and the kind of lasting change that you, as an author, can promise. Perhaps you'll recognize your reader, and yourself, among them.

Reader:
- I've experienced a chronic illness or a loss.
- I do not know how to reach the next level in my job.
- I'm losing my mind as a parent.
- I need to make more money.
- My anxiety is overwhelming my life.
- It is time for me to take control of my health.
- I struggle with relationships and connecting with others.
- I want the key to success that other people seem to have.

Author:
- I can tell you the secrets I've learned for coping with illness or loss.
- You can achieve the career of your dreams.
- There's a tool kit that every parent can use.
- You can gain lasting wealth so long as you know how.

- I'll help you find calm and satisfaction with your life.

- I'll teach you to eat better, live longer, or simply enjoy a healthy lifestyle.

- You will no longer feel alone.

- Here are the mindsets and practices of successful people.

What a reader takes away from your book is something agents and publishers need you to answer for them. It should be concrete for you when you conceive of your book, and you need to be able to explain it by the time you pitch it. If your reader is having a challenge of any kind, your book should offer a tangible solution. It's a simple equation of pain to gain.

TRY IT:

THE PAIN TO GAIN TRANSFORMATION

1. Grab your notepad (or laptop). Write out the words *pain* and *gain*.

2. Under the word *pain*, write the problem you think your reader faces.

3. Then, under *gain*, write the reward or change they will find upon reading your book. For fiction: Does your book provide an escape? Does it summon nostalgia? Will it transport them back or forward in time? All of these are valid "gains" for your readers.

The reader who understands their own problem isn't only who you're after. What may surprise you is that the most successful writers break through to the person who doesn't even know they have a problem. Best-selling author Mike Michalowicz anticipated a largely male audience of small business owners for the book that put him on the map: *Profit First.* When I spoke with him, he told me that what he didn't expect was the many stay at home moms who would come across his book on their husband's nightstand and pick it up, long having harbored their own dreams of entrepreneurship. In reviews and letters Mike received from these readers, women told him his book had validated them in ways their partners failed to—and they spread the word to their friends.

While this word of mouth kind of success can't exactly be engineered, when you land on the natural audience for your book, there can be a much wider reception that may surprise you. That value of understanding your "crossover" appeal will help to persuade agents of your book's true potential.

Other Genres

The pain to gain transformation is most discernible in self-help books, but memoirists and humorists often exploit a pain point to reach thousands of fans. Take David Sedaris, the essayist who writes about everything from traveling abroad to restaurant dining to common annoyances with family. His observational humor has made him a *New York Times* best-selling author and sought-after speaker. He touches on uncomfortable situations many of us have experienced and soothes us with his wit and playfulness, both transforming and delighting us.

Fiction writers use pain points to define and connect with readers as well. Shelby Van Pelt's novel *Remarkably Bright Creatures* features a protagonist named Tova who struggles with purpose and loneliness after the loss of her husband and son. That is, until she unexpectedly bonds with a curmudgeonly old octopus at the aquarium where she works. This unlikely friendship transforms Tova, teaching her about the depth of connection and reminding her of the beautiful things life still has to offer. The reader who has encountered grief and loss will be especially touched by this ethereal example.

Books give readers the opportunity to address the parts of themselves that need acknowledgment or healing. Have you ever picked up what you expected to be an easy beach read and walked away from it finding that it changed your perspective?

Even the title *Happy Place* by Emily Henry "had me thinking of my relationships and friendships" and "hit every emotion from happiness to sadness and everything in between,"[3] wrote one reader. A pitch alone can elicit a visceral reaction or the hint of an emotional consequence. Any book should tap into the core of who we are.

Delve Deep into a Fascinating Subject

Of course, as essential as pain and healing are to the human condition, not every reader wants to explore their pain! Sometimes we just want to learn more about a subject that fascinates us. Common examples of perennial subjects include political and military figures, gardening, cooking, and craft-making.

Editors are keen on narrative explorations that give practical guidance to readers. Usefulness has become the order of the day. And without this element, many editors today will pass. *How to Change Your Mind*, by Michael Pollan, uncovers what psychedelics can teach us about consciousness, dying, and addiction. He sorts through history to separate the myths from the truths about LSD and even embarks on a personal adventure of varying states of consciousness. One set of readers comes to this book because they are intrigued by psychedelics; another set comes to find a new means of experiencing the world. For each of these readers, Pollan's book provides value.

Or take best-selling author Kate Moore, who discovered the story of the "radium girls" while directing a play about them. Working in factory jobs that were once seen as coveted, these women learned they had been poisoned by dangerous, radioactive metals from the watches they painted. To protect others from a similar experience, they successfully sued their employer, creating the conditions for life-changing regulations and laws to be enacted and leading to a groundbreaking battle for workers' rights. Moore wrote the book she believed needed to exist to highlight these workers' valuable contributions to history. Not only does she inform her readers about a fascinating subject, but she also takes them on a harrowing real-life journey through time, including interviews with some of the women's families. While this book may have been seen as "niche," it's proven to have widespread appeal.

What topic do you wish to teach your reader about, and what new findings, facts, or insights will you illuminate for them? Whether your reader is brand new to your topic or a lifelong devotee, prepare to impress with something new and unexpected.

Entertain and Delight

If you look at the increasing popularity of thrillers and romance novels, it can be said that most of us look to literature to find entertainment and delight. This can look different depending on the reader. When I think about the novels I most want to sign, it's those that strike the balance between relatability and escape, humor and heart. They take me from a world I know deeply and transport me somewhere else entirely.

TRY IT:
DO YOU GIVE YOUR
READERS WHAT THEY WANT?

1. Does your book solve an urgent problem for readers? Circle Yes or No

2. Does your book take a deep dive into a subject of fascination?
   Circle Yes or No

3. Does your book entertain or delight?
   Circle Yes or No

We have now explored the three reasons a reader will pick a book off the shelf—it solves a problem, speaks to a subject of fascination, or simply delights the senses. Now it's your turn to decipher what your particular book promises to the person who doesn't know you.

Meet Your Readers

One might think that as the former editor-in-chief of *Seventeen*, Ann Shoket, had the clout, connections, and experience in journalism to get a book deal based on her credentials alone. But when she decided to take the next step in her career and write a book, she didn't want to write the obvious tome about her own life and career. She wanted to contribute something meaningful and powerful for the young women who had followed her for nearly a decade at *Seventeen*. While working in magazines, she had focused on their teenage years, but to help these women, who were now young professionals, she would have to prove to editors that she still understood these women and could meet them where they were now in their journey.

So Ann tried an experiment. Instead of going out in the field to conduct research, she brought the research to her. Every month, rotating groups of professional women—friends of friends, word-of-mouth connections—were invited to her kitchen table to enjoy gourmet pizza, rosé, and conversation. They talked through work, passion, respect, money, relationships, and "the kind of stuff that you can't ask your boss." They came together to support each other, trade notes, and share insider secrets.

Through these dinners, Ann became intimately familiar with the challenges of these women—and how she could help them. She paid close attention to the questions they asked and the language they used to describe their struggles. Those discussions became a research study and the foundation of her book *The Big Life*. In it, Ann teaches how to craft a career you love, get respect for your work, find the people who will support you, and even start a side hustle. It was at one of these dinners that I first met Ann and came to represent her as a speaker.

Today *The Big Life* isn't just a book; it's a popular keynote and a vibrant online community. None of this would have been possible without Ann being so plugged in to her target demographic. The detailed notes she took from her dozens of dinner conversations provided her future editor with the "data" needed to acquire her book—for a compelling amount!

Jenny Jackson, vice president and executive editor at Knopf and *New York Times* best-selling author of the novel *Pineapple Street*, told me that when she reads fiction pitches, she has specific readers in mind. Perhaps it's her college roommate in the Midwest, her 70-year-old mom, or a member of her book club. But what clinches the deal is when Jenny instinctively knows that one of her authors will love the book she's considering enough to write a **blurb** for it. You too need this intimate knowledge of your reader to write a book that succeeds.

In fact, if you are fortunate enough to meet with publishers, they will plainly ask: "Who do you see as the reader for the book?" Understanding what it is you need to validate for your intended reader and what they crave will provide more clues to honing your big idea. If you can't prove any relevance to your reader, you have missed a pivotal piece.

You know your reader better than you think you do. They are probably a lot like you, because so many of you are writing the book you've always looked for but couldn't find on Amazon or bookshelves.

A quick aside: for novelists, it may be that you are taking readers on an adventure. When you conceive of a book as an adventure, you can stave off what we call interiority—the quality of living inside just one character's mind. Most readers today do not have the attention span to keep engaged in the emotions and thoughts of a single character unless the writing is of exceedingly rare and sharp quality. Too much interiority can damage your chances of breaking through to agents. Instead, I advise novelists looking to publish commercially to demonstrate plot-forward, propulsive narratives in their pitch that are full of surprises, twists, and turns or high stakes that keep a reader glued to their seat.

Whether you're transporting someone on the journey of your own life or creating a fantastical, immersive universe we've never seen before, your reader needs to be spoken to on every page. "You have a precious moment with a reader when they sit down and interact with you through the book one-on-one. You can really change how they live and what they think—their take on the world," said Stephanie Frerich, vice president and executive editor at Simon & Schuster.

If a book fails to capture a reader's interest, they will put it down and move on. And then they certainly won't tell their friends about it, offer a positive review, or buy it for others—the upward spiral that creates long-tail sales, which agents and editors look for above everything else.

TRY IT:
YOUR READER AVATAR

What qualities does your typical reader have?
Answer these questions to the best of your ability.

Age range

Profession

Hobbies or interests

Strong distastes

What have they always wanted?

What would they never do?

What keeps them up at night?

Anything else (certain authors will know everything
down to their Enneagram type!)

So far, we've covered your big idea, how to use comparative titles, and who your reader is. These elements are imperative to a strong query, but they're not all that matters. Your voice and authority as our narrator are just as important. Now that you have an idea of who your book is for and how it serves them, let that inform how you prove to agents and readers that you are a trustworthy guide. That's what we'll cover in Step 4.

STEP 4

Claim Your Authority

Dear Lucinda,
I'm writing a memoir, but I'm not a known author.
Is there any hope that I'll still be published?
— MARCUS (QUEENS, NY)

One of the biggest insecurities I hear from the writers I teach is that they will be seen as imposters. When you take that first action to submit your work to an agent, it's incredibly nerve-racking. You are putting yourself on a stage, waiting for everyone to see through you. My own experience of this was as a child opera singer at the Metropolitan Opera, standing next to Luciano Pavarotti. For you, it's being an unknown thriller writer standing next to Lee Child. Or a hopeful memoirist comparing yourself to Dani Shapiro. Best-selling author Colette Baron-Reid said, "I popped a rib from terror in the beginning because I was so scared I didn't have anything original to say."

Here's the thing: you don't have to have an advanced degree, write for *The New Yorker*, or have 20 years of experience in your field to write a life-changing book. If you do, that will certainly help, but no matter what you possess or lack, you must have vision. This step is about cultivating the mindset that you will be an author, no matter what or how long it takes.

BUILD YOUR CREDIBILITY

When I discovered 22-year-old Chris Bailey, he had a popular blog called *The Productivity Project*, that was swiftly gaining a following. Right out of college, he had turned down lucrative job offers to spend a year performing a deep-dive experiment into a subject he had been enamored with since he was a teenager: productivity.

He hadn't queried us—instead he had attracted the notice of one of our authors, who suggested we approach him about a book. When I did reach out via Twitter (now X), it was a life-changing moment for us both. He loved writing, and he had found great reward engaging a community of enthusiasts around his thought-provoking and practical ideas. When I asked for his role model, he had an immediate answer: "I want to be David Allen."

"For millennials," I added.

The thought that he could write a book and potentially create a living by diving deep into a subject he loved—without taking on a graduate degree or a conventional corporate job—was alluring to Chris. His big idea was to read every productivity book and try every experiment out there—cutting out caffeine and sugar, digitally unplugging, living in isolation—to test what worked best.

While his proven audience wasn't huge, he had a fan following online that was visibly engaging with his ideas and talent for quirky storytelling.

The Productivity Project launched Chris as a best-selling author of three books published with Penguin Random House and translated into over 40 languages. His blog and e-mail list have increased exponentially. He speaks and consults for companies frequently, commanding large fees. And he has a podcast where he gets to sit down with other popular authors and thought leaders to continue in his learning and teaching.

Chris was not an expert with decades of experience in the workforce. He didn't have an advanced degree. He wasn't a recognized leader in his field. But by studying all the academic literature, he was able to create an appealing body of work around his interests and offer a fresh perspective. This gave him credibility—he became someone readers could trust. What he exhibited as a first-time author was, in a word, authority. His success resulted from becoming an expert in his own right.

If you are looking to establish yourself as an expert, what's holding you back from becoming it on your own? Pedigree can help, but it isn't everything. There is no substitute for a personal connection to your idea. Readers love when you are the guinea pig for them. As Chris puts it: "My best book ideas are usually born out of my efforts and struggles and are always based on research and my own experiences. If I'm struggling with something, other people likely are too. And if I learn interesting things in overcoming those struggles, other people will probably benefit just the same."

In an attempt to decrease clutter and consumption in her life, my client Cait Flanders implemented a two-year shopping ban for herself, documenting what she learned on social media and her blog. She realized that the poor financial choice of buying things when she needed a mental boost was preventing her from living the creativity-rich and clutter-free life she yearned for. As she cut unnecessary purchases, alcohol, and television from her life, the process revealed deeper challenges and lessons about what really mattered to her in the larger scheme of life. Cait shared it all with a growing audience of people who suspected they had the same habits. She practiced what she preached, and in doing so endeared herself to the thousands who came eagerly to what became the best-selling book *The Year of Less*.

Like Chris or Cait, your authenticity can be your authority. Because, really, what we mean when we talk about "authority" or "credibility" is: Do you have the capacity to be trusted? Trust is derived when others feel a genuine connection. Whether or not you are a social media celebrity with millions of followers, readers are drawn to writers who are honest about their lives and learnings and share the straightforward truth.

YOUR LIVED EXPERIENCE IS YOUR EXPERTISE

My client Michelle Dowd wrote one of the most popular *New York Times* "Modern Love" columns of 2020, which I came across while reading the paper one weekend. Immediately I thought, *This woman has a voice.* I was one of several agents who reached out to see if she was interested in writing a book. Michelle grew up on a mountain in the Angeles National Forest, raised by an ultra-religious apocalyptic cult run by her grandfather. Her family and their followers believed that they must prepare themselves to survive the imminent end of the world. Her memoir, *Forager: Field Notes for Surviving a Family Cult,* describes her experience growing up and eventually finding the strength to break free.

Many writers balk at the term "expert." The thing is: you are an expert in your own life experiences. Your lived experience is your expertise, and this is especially true for those of you who are older with rich life experiences to draw from and wisdom to share with others. If you are beginning this journey later in life, agents, editors, and readers will respect the percipience that comes with age. Think of Pulitzer Prize–winning memoirist Frank McCourt, who published *Angela's Ashes* when he was 68 and retired. Anne Youngson wrote her first novel, *Meet Me at the Museum,* when she was 69. Youngson admitted in *The Guardian* that at first she saw her age as a commercial disadvantage but soon realized that she had a better sense of herself exactly because she was older.[4]

Age can be an asset. Your wealth of insights becomes your credibility, a reason readers will have confidence in you.

WHEN YOU ARE A RECOGNIZED EXPERT

Rebecca Heiss was a professor and scientist with a Ph.D. in biology long before her query letter came my way. She was pitching a book about the blind spots we encounter in the working world and beyond as a result of our "stone-aged brains" struggling to operate in a modern environment. *Instinct: Rewire Your Brain with Science-Backed Solutions to Increase Productivity and Achieve Success* began as a collection of her popular keynotes translated into prose, providing insightful solutions for employers and employees alike.

Rebecca had a smart idea and the credentials to support her argument, which, despite a nascent social media following or e-mail list, helped convince me to represent her and a publisher to eventually take her on. But more than that, she did two other things well. She incorporated humor and compelling personal stories into her work, which showed a softer, less academic side. "My agent encouraged me not to let my expertise stand in the way of sharing my personal experiences," recalled Adam Grant in our interview. "One of the most memorable suggestions he gave me was to write like I teach, not like I write research papers. That's been transformative for me as a writer—it closed the distance between me and the reader."

Rebecca was also a regular speaker with the industriousness and vision of a serious promoter. Dorie Clark, author of *The Long Game* and *Stand Out*, among others, put it this way: "Being recognized as an expert is necessary but not sufficient to land a nonfiction book deal. You're a far more attractive candidate when you can convince publishers that you can market effectively."

But how does one make the leap from expert in their field to a widely seen thought leader or a writer by trade? Any of these applications can do the trick—and will also be helpful later on when querying. (Good news: you need not accomplish them all.)

- An award-winning essay or short story
- An article in a notable publication
- Media attention
- Work experience with a widely known company (nonfiction)
- Endorsements from well-known authors

- Experience at a reputable institution or company (nonfiction)
- An MFA (fiction or narrative)
- An award of any kind
- Tutelage under a well-recognized author or mentor
- A proprietary framework (nonfiction)
- Frequent speaking and consulting engagements (nonfiction)
- A large social media following or e-mail list

Possessing any of the above accolades will up the ante as you are evaluated by agents as an author with a career ahead.

YOUR FUTURE SELF

In speaking with editors and publishers, Chris Bailey learned that a book was just one part of the picture. A book of note can give way to an even more lucrative speaking career, consulting, online programs, and more.

Some authors hesitate to envision all of this—their audience, their speaking circuit, a book's publicity—because it's so early in the process. Your book could be just a Word document at this stage! But having a long-term vision, confidence, and believable authority on your topic is exactly what's needed to persuade an agent or publisher.

Vision signifies your long-term commitment to writing. Right now you are primarily concerned with getting one book published, not necessarily starting a new career. But flip this around. If you could have a career as

GET SIGNED

an author, what would your first book be? And on the success of that first book, what could your follow-up books become? If your debut is your "pilot," it helps to have the whole series in mind. Agents and editors shy away from a one-hit wonder.

If you are a novelist, do you have more novels in you? If you're an entrepreneur, can your book be a tool to grow your business and vice versa? For memoirists, could your story become a feature film? Will your self-help message be so inspirational that it will start a movement? Or maybe your reported narrative shines a light on a devastating problem, and you'll become a sought-after spokesperson for creating a change in the world

If you have the chance to meet with an editor one day, they may want to hear about your "five-year plan" and beyond. Don't think of this as a job interview, just begin by reflecting on those you admire. It's the way that most of us, including me, mold our careers. The person who finally took a chance on me when no one else would was an agent named Christy Fletcher. Her ambition and work ethic astounded me. She was at her desk from nine or ten in the morning until eight or nine at night, all with two small children at home. As a mother now, I understand this sacrifice. Everyone else took long lunches with editors, but not Christy. It was too important that she be at her desk, advocating for her authors, reading new pitches, and searching for the next great talent.

You too need role models. Meeting them in person, while beneficial, is no longer required. Learn much of what you need to know about an author just by googling or consuming their content. Almost every successful author is a public personality, visible in some way. Follow them,

72

read them, listen to them, study them, and draw courage and inspiration from their example. Joan Didion once remarked that she would type out Ernest Hemingway's stories just to learn how he constructed sentences. There are many ways to study mentors from afar.

A few questions that I'll often ask a writer who I'm considering taking on are: What authors do you admire and consider your contemporaries? Do you wish to spend all of your time writing or most of your time promoting? Do you see a speaking career for yourself? A podcast? Legendary former executive editor at Viking Rick Kot said that the ideal situation for publishers is to have an author who will reliably publish a novel every year. Envision that one day this could be you.

What I'm asking is that you step into your Future Self, because every one of your role models, I assure you, started unknown. What about your character or your intentions aligns you with those authors you aspire to be? As an entrepreneur who has studied and been inspired by the entrepreneurs I represent, my mantra has always been: "I'm building an empire!" This has always been my affirmation as a business owner and entrepreneur. It's what I remind myself of when the days feel long and the progress slow. If you don't currently feel confident to proclaim, "I am," you can always substitute with "I will" or "I am going to." But make it authoritative. You need to believe it before anyone else will.

TRY IT:
DECLARE YOUR FUTURE SELF

Grab a notebook or open up a blank document on your computer and think through these prompts.

1. If there were one author you could be, who would you choose? Why?

2. Describe three characteristics of that person's voice on the page.

3. Describe three characteristics of that person's voice in podcast interviews or social media.

4. What does this author's career look like now, after having a successful book—or more than one? (Answers could be: speaker, podcaster, journalist, full-time writer.)

Now that you've stepped fearlessly into your potential, the next step in your journey to get signed is to get *seen* by the industry. Whether you can't wait to hone your marketing skills or you're avoiding promotion like the plague, the following chapter will give you the confidence to amplify your voice and your message.

STEP 5

Get Seen

Dear Lucinda,
I keep hearing that I need to have a platform.
But I hate social media and promoting myself.
Is that the only way to get published?

— MATT (TALLAHASSEE, FL)

Who wants to be a self-promoter?

No one.

This is just not what most writers got into the trade to become. Was there ever a time that an author did not have to be a marketer to get a book deal? According to agents and editors who have been in the business for over 30 years, there was. Kathy Robbins, founder of the literary agency the Robbins Office in New York, said, "Before the advent of the Internet and social media, authors had neither platforms nor followers, because such things didn't exist. Publicity consisted of reviews, features, radio and TV appearances, and author tours. An author being 'promotable' was an asset. But not determining."

But at the very moment Lucinda Literary was founded in 2011, everything was changing—for better and for worse. Gretchen Rubin's *The Happiness Project*, among other hit titles, showed publishers that the Internet was fertile ground for authors to plant a stake and gather a thriving community of followers around their work. The Internet provided a portal between authors and readers that was unparalleled by traditional media because it allowed for constant dialogue. And the power of social media to amplify an author's voice and message was discovered shortly thereafter.

In this chapter, you will find a tactic, medium, or strategy that works for you. Whether you're an introvert or extrovert, writers of all personality types get book deals every day. Like everything else in the publishing process, it's a matter of leaning in to your strengths.

WHAT IS A PLATFORM?

Let me bring you back to the three keys to getting an agent and a book deal. The first is the potential we will see in your big idea. The second is the potential we'll see in your writing (this often comes down to craft, which is beyond the scope of this book, but crucial for you to always be developing). The third is your platform.

In his search for an agent, Paul Jarvis, a future agency client, approached me with a genius idea: a book with a refreshingly original business strategy that prioritized being "better" over "bigger." Paul didn't have any official credentials. He wasn't a Ph.D., had not worked within a big corporation, and neither spoke nor consulted for companies. He actually hated public speaking! It wasn't in his career plan.

But in addition to a big idea, the first key, he also had the third key: a platform. (And a quick reminder: you only need two!) Paul had been writing and publicly experimenting with his ideas for years. As one of the first developers of an online course, Paul had amassed a large e-mail list and Twitter (now X) following, unusual for an introverted web designer. With an engaged following around his work, he could ask anything of his audience and receive meaningful answers. He could dialogue with those primed to embrace, or already embarking upon, his "return to roots" business philosophy. He could basically do his own research in real time.

That electrifying instinct I had about Paul's future commercial success proved true. His proposal for a book called *Company of One* was sold to a major publisher at auction. It has since gone on to earn **royalties** and translation deals in 12 languages. Paul's clamoring global fan base came ready to buy and endorse his work when the book was released and continually over time. In fact, having a book behind him exponentially increased his following, as we see for so many authors. That is the advantage of a platform, and it's what every agent wants.

Here's a simple way to see it:

EXISTING AUDIENCE
+
POTENTIAL REACH
=
PLATFORM

Audience

In today's competitive publishing landscape, it can be critical to demonstrate an engaged and built-in audience, a community of individuals bound together by shared interests or values. These are the people who are paying attention to you and already consuming your work. If you were to launch your book today, who would buy it? Most obvious to publishers and agents will be those with whom you are already in conversation.

If you're a speaker for corporations, your audience is executives. If you're a psychologist or healing practitioner, it's your clients—whether it's those you see in person or those who take your courses. If you're a self-help expert, it could be your podcast or social media following. If you're a literary writer, it's typically those who read your bylines in various publications, but it could also be those in your writing group or book club who share your tastes.

Reach

Inspirational author of *You Are the Medicine*, Asha Frost, tried a different approach than sticking to one group. She increased her readers by saying yes to everything: every podcast, summit, and appearance—all of which had different audiences. This translated to what agents see as reach: exposure that alludes to awareness, engagement, and community around your work. Think of it as access. It's the organizations, networks, reviewers, media, authors, and other influencers that support you.

Audience and reach, which together comprise platform, are often directly tied to how an author's potential is assessed, especially for nonfiction writers.

The most tangible evidence of a platform is social media, but agents and editors actually use a combination of elements to evaluate your overall sales potential—many of which aren't as obvious. Platform can be any of the following. A combination of any of these accomplishments will be judged most favorably by the industry.

- An engaged online following (50,000+) on a single platform
- A popular blog (50,000+ monthly hits)
- Major media attention
- A "name" company that you lead or work for
- A growing and engaged e-mail list (25,000+)
- A podcast that's received many downloads or reviews (yours or an appearance on someone else's—50,000+)
- Regular teachings or workshops to a growing audience
- Regular speaking engagements (20+ events per year)
- A course with many successful and happy students (25,000+ purchases)
- A network of authors or influencers who can endorse your work*

Your credentials, as discussed in Step 4, are also part of your platform. Sometimes they can even stand in place of the criteria above. If you are not a well-connected-promoter type, you should still feel confident in your inherent

---

*   *Threshold numbers are approximations at the time of writing this book.*

knowledge or your topic, as proven within elements such as:

- An advanced degree
- Previous experience writing for notable publications
- A teaching affiliation or relevant graduate work

This diverse array of qualifications that shows you have an audience for your work gives you so much more to consider beyond TikTok. This should be great news for those of you uninterested in learning about hashtags and algorithms.

Agents and editors will not necessarily see all that you bring to the table through Internet research (which is the very first thing we do if we are intrigued by your idea). There's a bigger picture you need to paint for how you are known. "Tell me what Google hasn't" is a prompt I give prospective clients in trying to learn more about their recognition and activity. What are you doing behind the scenes to reach the people whom you hope will be your readers? Do you speak regularly, have devoted e-mail subscribers, or sell online products that attract downloads into the thousands? Did you have a viral reaction to a podcast interview? Don't leave it to our imagination to guess.

The examples above prove existing connections to a wide or highly engaged audience. No one likes marketing that is bragging or self-aggrandizing, so if that's how you have perceived the process of building a platform, it's time to reframe your thinking. In fact, as you'll see, the most successful writers do just the opposite and share their insights generously with humility instead of grandstanding. Getting seen is about attracting a like-minded coalition that supports one another.

YOUR VCO

"So now I know what a platform is, but how do I go about building one?" This is a common refrain. For those already putting themselves out there, the better question to ask is: "What are the ways I might want to rethink or optimize my platform to better support my chances of a successful book?"

A carefully conceived platform includes not all people but the right people—your future readers. As Colette Baron-Reid poignantly told me, "Nobody's ever heard of Motörhead, but their stadiums and merchandise sell out because their fans know about them. I don't care if everybody knows me. I just want to serve the people that want to be served by me. I want to be Motörhead."

If you have name recognition as a yoga teacher, from popular YouTube videos to a large e-mail list, that will serve you incredibly well when you want to write a book about yoga. But if you decide to write in a category you're not known for, like fiction, you will have a harder time persuading agents and editors that a novel will appeal to your yoga fans. How can we be sure those fans will follow you to a new concept or modality they've never seen from you before?

To build the right platform for your book, whether you're a children's writer, a biographer, or a clinician, you will need to establish what I call your VCO. VCO stands for voice, content, and offering. And there are different ways in which it applies to both fiction and nonfiction authors.

YOUR "VCO"

VOICE	CONTENT	OFFERING
Your personality and presentation (written, audio, or visuals)	What you want to talk about	What you can give readers

Your **voice** is what is most authentic about your personality and worldview—it puts a unique stamp on the work you create and should come through in every medium. You'll remember my client Cait, who wrote the *Wall Street Journal* bestseller *The Year of Less*. She is known for being warm, genuine, heartfelt, and deep-thinking. So too is her voice. A reader commented, "Reading your writing is like breathing the freshest air and standing on a mountain of gentle perspective. Welcoming, curiosity-inspiring, kind." That describes Cait and her writing perfectly. Voice, simply, is where you get to be you.

Your platform is an opportunity to make new connections by finding a voice that transcends what's possible on the page. Leading with your voice, there's an opportunity to convert hundreds of strangers into your greatest fans—quite literally, when you consider that audiovisual mediums are the preferred mode of content consumption online. For some authors, this frees them to save the written work for the page. For other authors, sharing your voice in text form is more comfortable and can be equally effective. There is no right or wrong way to do this. A remarkable voice can make the most skeptical publisher interested, discounting other weaknesses in your platform. Agents and editors often assess if they find your voice to be distinctive online before they even look at your pages.

Can AI Create My Voice for Me?

There's no doubt that artificial intelligence will continue to drastically alter every field in which humans work. As authors and editors, AI can complement our gifts to readers and serve as a thought partner or a second eye in any sort of content we create.

But even with the aid of computer science, the craft of writing is so bespoke, so personal to our experience and our imagination, that I can't imagine artificial intelligence replacing who we are and what we do as writers. And because it doesn't know you inside out as you know yourself—the intricacies of your platform or the promise in your big idea—it cannot write the best pitch for you either.

Your **content** is the material you send out into the ether, and it needs to reflect subjects that you regularly speak to and that surround your book. It's ideal when you can be responsive to the news of the day, which means you don't have to feel pressure around creating original content every time. Much like books, subject matter tends to strike a chord when it's either timely (such as commentary on a trend) or timeless (like an inspirational quote or infographic containing perennial wisdom). And of course, like books, the best content does both. Whatever you do, avoid the trap of solely showcasing your "GPL"—your glossy, perfect life. Cait Flanders credits the platform she has built to a vulnerability that she courageously shared with her community. She strikes her fans as an approachable best friend who genuinely cares about their challenges and is willing to share her own with transparency in return. Engage in a raw and human way, and you will see much bigger gains than trying to be something you are not. People—including agents and editors—can sniff out a fake.

Your **offering** shouldn't be confused with a product. It's more like a gift or resource, the clear benefit for why anyone would follow your work to begin with, and in this way, it's intrinsically connected to what will become your book. It's your value proposition. For practical nonfiction writers, this might be obvious. Maybe your offering is that you teach your audience public speaking or how to get organized. But it can be much more than this. For years, Cait spoke to the power of minimalism on her blog and podcast—from how to live on a shoestring budget to how to declutter your home to how to give up a home entirely. But her greater gift was calm. Reduction. Levity. In our pitch letter to publishers, we described her memoir as "a book for women who want to think deeply and live lightly." A memoir student of ours defined his offering as "a community to amplify diverse voices and those who have suffered trauma." In bearing his life story, he offers people a place to feel heard, be seen, and know they are no longer alone.

Young adult novelist Alice Oseman navigates readers through growing up, changing, and searching for one's identity. Peter Heller takes us on adventures in nature. Voice, content, and offering coalesce. They are intimately interwoven. Your VCO will distinguish you to readers.

Now let's determine your voice, content, and offering and, most important, how they fit together.

TRY IT: FIND YOUR "VCO"

VOICE: Imagine you've been asked to appear on a famous podcast to promote your book. What is the nature of the podcast? Is it funny and lighthearted? Academic and cerebral? Scientific or focused on personal development? What kind of questions would the interviewer ask you? Imagining the type of interview you might attract can help you to determine your voice and how the public will hear it.

Three words that describe your voice:

1.

2.

3.

CONTENT: As you spend time on the social media feeds of the authors in your space whom you admire, look specifically at the elements that draw you to someone. Is it their social commentary on news related to your industry? Or is it musings on their personal life? You don't need to (and shouldn't) copy another author exactly, but it's helpful to figure out what *you* enjoy consuming as a way to determine what your followers might enjoy too.

Write down three topics that you genuinely enjoy posting and writing about:

1.

2.

3.

OFFERING: Ultimately, what is the experience you want readers to have as they engage with you? What do you want them to feel, learn, or leave with? If you're writing a prescriptive nonfiction book, your takeaway should be obvious (e.g., "learn to grow from trauma"), but if you're writing narrative nonfiction or fiction, this can be something akin to "experience life through someone else's eyes" or "become immersed in an adventurous love story." Your offering should deliver on the same promise as your book. Think back to Step 3, when you defined your reader. What is the most valuable thing you can give that person? In one sentence, jot this down.

My Offering is:

ROAD TESTING YOUR VCO ONLINE

There are two primary ways in which publishers view platform: how you engage with possible readers for your proposed book online, in the digital world, and how you engage with them "offline," in the analog world. There's an overlap between the two, and in just a bit, we will examine the myriad ways in which these two categories break down. Because online platform is the most immediately visible to publishers, let's begin there. This is where you can put your VCO to the test and lean in to experimentation. You will start small, so don't worry about making mistakes. Because, in fact, there are no mistakes. You will need to refine your VCO until it's unique, sharp, and resonant.

"But how can I know what will resonate?" writers often ask. And here's where the obvious becomes easy to overlook: let someone tell you.

In addition to your most skeptical but supportive best friend (I have mine on speed dial), ask your audience or the people in your network, big or small. What kind of help, or story, are they looking for? Probe what they like most about what and how you communicate. At some point you will begin to see engagement with your questions and more and more people chiming in to provide answers. If you don't want to ask them a question directly, pay attention to your comments and shares. What seems to be getting the most traction? Are people passing your ideas around? Are they replying to you and others? That's when you know your VCO is working. And you are demonstrating to agents, editors, and even film producers that people are coming to you for your unique contribution.

Road Test Your VCO through Short-Form Writing

First-time author Kristen Roupenian's short story "Cat Person" went viral in *The New Yorker* and led to a reported $1.2 million deal for the anthology *You Know You Want This*, which included "Cat Person." Similarly, the hit novel *Normal People*, by Sally Rooney, began as a short story titled "At the Clinic," originally published in the UK-based journal the *White Review*. This is great evidence that even if your audience has consumed this exact content before, they will still want to buy it. Don't be afraid of offering too much for free, as your true fans will pay money for your work no matter what.

But writing something for a large publication isn't the only way to test out your big idea. Mark Manson's mega-bestseller *The Subtle Art of Not Giving a F*ck* was an article on his own blog that went viral before it became a book. An interesting fact about that: before Manson even decided to create the article, it was just a catchy title he had spinning in his brain for almost a year. His assistant found it in a "blog post ideas" document and suggested he write it. It was a contrarian take on self-help (which became Manson's entire brand)—that not caring about certain people and things and not trying so hard makes all the difference. The moment the piece appeared on his blog, thousands of people began to share it on social media. This was all the evidence he needed that he had landed on something that people were clamoring for.

Trying something publicly is a great way to get instant feedback. This can feel nerve-wracking to writers, but deliberate practice and workshopping your idea in community with others is arguably the best way to find it. Building your platform can be done both online and off.

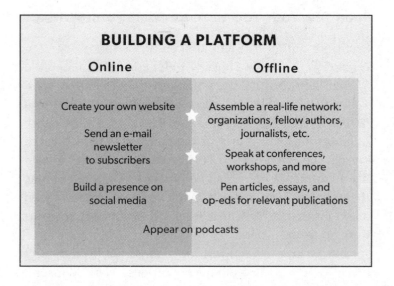

BUILDING A PLATFORM

Online	Offline
Create your own website	Assemble a real-life network: organizations, fellow authors, journalists, etc.
Send an e-mail newsletter to subscribers	Speak at conferences, workshops, and more
Build a presence on social media	Pen articles, essays, and op-eds for relevant publications
Appear on podcasts	

You don't actually need very much to get started. You can road test your VCO by beginning with something even simpler than getting published in a publication or writing on your blog. My client Ron Friedman regularly sends surveys to solicit feedback on new book ideas or events he's looking to launch. Those surveys will either corroborate his interests or reveal surprising new directions for his next project. Either way, he will glean what his audience wants most from him.

Even if your following is small, the engagement that you will eventually see will provide agents and publishers with "proof of concept," evidence that people are interested in your idea. Show that your concept can create a conversation, and more modest platform numbers become less of an obstacle. Now let's look at ways to build those numbers.

THE 3 BUILDING BLOCKS FOR CREATING A DIGITAL EMPIRE

With your distinct VCO and evidence of how your message serves your audience, you have everything you need to thrive online. Below, I've listed what I see as the basic pieces to establishing yourself online: a website, an e-mail list, and a social media presence. While these aren't strict requirements for getting signed, all authors can benefit from this foundation that will serve another purpose—marketing their books successfully later on. This is how you build the mountain so they will come.

WEBSITE + E-MAIL LIST + SOCIAL MEDIA = DIGITAL EMPIRE

WEBSITE

E-MAIL NEWSLETTER LIST

SOCIAL MEDIA PRESENCE

Set up a basic professional website. Include your bio, option to subscribe to your e-mail list, and an overview of your work.

Make a schedule (whether daily, weekly, or monthly) and stick to it. Think of it like e-mailing a group of friends.

Post consistent content that your followers can expect to benefit from or simply enjoy.

Your Website

Writers are surprised to learn that even before publishing a book, you can—even should—have a website. Having a professional website is a hallmark of expertise. This can be bare bones and may or may not be what you will ultimately use to promote your book. Just a simple, clean website with a bio, an overview of your work, a way to get in touch with you, and a page to sign up for your newsletter is really all that's needed. Many of our authors have created these for themselves for free.

Much of what I recommend in this chapter are suggestions, options from which to choose. But to look like a professional author and curate what agents and publishers will see, a website can't be recommended more highly for nonfiction writers and novelists alike. And there's no need to wait until you have a book out on shelves. Peruse the websites of authors you look up to, and mimic what you like most. Then give your website your own unique twist. At GetSignedBook.com, you can find more guidance and recommended resources.

Your "List"

While not seen by agents as essential for fiction writers, an e-mail list, known simply in the industry as a "list," is possibly the most compelling asset that any writer can bring to the table. It also means that authors who prefer to be more private can do what they love—writing—as opposed to being more public on social media.

Your e-mail list is usually built by sending out a regular newsletter. Don't be daunted: think of this as an e-mail update you're sending to a bunch of friends. It can be daily, weekly, or monthly, and it can be any length or topic. Hay House, the publisher of this book, estimates that 30 percent of someone's e-mail list, on average, will convert into book buyers. At best. This means that if your newsletter is 100 people, only 30 will have reasonably bought your book. Now you know why we're looking for such a high subscriber count.

Unlike social media, you own your e-mail list. If Facebook is shut down tomorrow, you could lose all of your followers and no longer be able to reach them. But with your readers' e-mail addresses, you can always stay in touch, and most essential, *these are people who have opted in to hear from you.* The people who sign up to be on your e-mail list can be your most ardent supporters. Landing in someone's inbox is more intimate and meaningful than being a transient, noncommittal social media follower.

This is very good news for many writers who hate the idea of being public on social media. A newsletter allows you to do what you do best: write—and be creative!—about subject lines, topics, stories you wish to tell, and all the books and other authors you want your people to know. Contrary to what you might be thinking, this will not (or it shouldn't) take over your day job. It's just about being disciplined enough to give it some measure of your time, consistently.

Offer Something for Free

The best way to start and grow an e-mail list is to offer people a gift or resource for joining called a "lead magnet." I'm dismayed when I see writers spending valuable time creating long, meaningful articles or personal essays on their blogs that elude the views they hope for simply because they do not have a compelling reason for someone to sign up to their list. A prompt that says "Subscribe to my newsletter!" is unlikely to draw in those who don't know you. Some of you in the entrepreneurial or business space may be familiar with the power of lead magnets. Here are a few quick ideas:

- If you are an academic, offer a white paper or in-depth thought-leadership piece that describes your data and perspective.

- Entrepreneurs and self-help experts can share inspiration or lessons via an e-book or link to a talk you gave.

- Create a quiz to test something about your audience and provide them with results when they sign up.

- Fiction writers often give away a short story, first chapter to a book, or a cheat sheet to understand the fantasy world you've created.

- Share an article with an irresistible hook that can be accessed only through your website and hasn't been shared elsewhere.

- Offer a template of some sort (goals, grocery list, experiments, fitness workouts, etc.).

- Create a list of resources your audience might want (e.g., "10 Apps I Use Every Day").

The truth is, for anyone looking to build an e-mail list, a lead magnet could exponentially increase your numbers, which will also tell you whether or not your offering is working. Before he landed his first book deal, Ben Hardy built an e-mail list of over 200,000 people by linking them to a simple free e-book about time-hacking at the end of all his Medium posts. The size of this list helped him secure a six-figure book deal as a first-time author.

Your Social Media

Do I need to be present on all social media outlets? Sometimes the thought of running multiple social media handles makes authors want to die a little inside. I understand. As creatives, you just want to do the writing and leave the marketing and platform-building to someone else. While social media, at the time of writing this book, remains less powerful than a large or engaged e-mail list in terms of converting followers into book buyers, a social media presence can still help significantly when it comes to getting an agent. For those interested, I want to make sure we cover it briefly.

Let me relieve a little pressure first: no, you do not have to be on every single social media platform. It is a good idea to aim for at least two to three platforms, like TikTok,

X (formerly Twitter) and Threads, Instagram, Facebook, You-Tube, or LinkedIn. But really, you want to dominate one to two platforms and use them religiously to grow a thriving community. Poet Rupi Kaur built a huge following exclusively on Instagram well before her best-selling book *Milk and Honey* was published. She simply began publishing poems regularly, and her followers shared them on their platforms. If you haven't yet committed to a social media strategy, consider first where your target audience hangs out.

Here are just a few ways authors are using social media effectively and tips for using it:

Be authentic to you.

Sharing other people's posts will only get you so far. In order to really cultivate an audience, you need to bring your unique VCO to the table.

Think beyond your own opinions.

Content that encourages interaction, such as quizzes and giveaways, or invites insights from other people tends to gain traction easily.

Be conversational with other players in your space.

Mentioning other people in posts (assuming they are willing to be mentioned or have agreed to endorse you) helps to further widen both your audience and that of the person mentioned.

Experiment with visuals.

Visual media is consistently more popular than text. Free tools like Canva are great for making simple yet striking visuals to accompany your posts. Videos can just be filmed from your phone—the less formal, the better!

Think ahead to save you time.

Programs like Hootsuite help to schedule social media posts so you don't have to write one every single day. Draft, schedule, and sit back! There are definitely benefits to posting "in the moment," but it also helps to have regular content on auto-play so you can focus on book writing.

Attach your posts to the trends that will spark conversation.

When you touch upon a wider trend in your content, use hashtags to amplify your message for those searching on that topic.

Promote free resources.

The word *free* is powerful, but only use it when you mean it. Make sure the resources you promote are truly complementary and valuable. Trust is something easily broken and hard to rebuild if you advertise something that turns out not to be true or live up to its promise.

Manage the haters with grace.

Handle criticism with dignity. Filter and be thoughtful when you choose to respond to negative feedback.

Think before you post.

Protect your digital footprint and be deliberate about what you decide to post. Agents and editors will notice if your content is overly controversial or offensive. Editors will look for whether or not authors have been publicly maligned or are known for spreading misinformation over any given number of followers.

Can't I hire someone to do this for me? It's a question I'm so often asked by writers daunted by social media. You can, but most of our successful authors will personally create content for at least one feed themselves, as it's difficult to have someone clone you in a video (I haven't seen that one yet)! This doesn't mean you need to handle all the responding yourself, and you can certainly outsource posting on platforms that interest you less.

We have seen countless writers hire social media managers and not see the kind of growth or engagement necessary to secure a publishing deal. My advice is this: do your research and be clear about what you want to gain from that hire and how delegating execution allows *you* to create the best content. Also, set reasonable expectations—it takes time to build a following!

REUSE AND RECYCLE: THE ULTIMATE PLATFORM-BUILDING HACK

You may now be asking, *But how much content do I need to create here? I'm already writing a book!* Yes, good content creation takes time and effort, but the best shortcut I've found is repurposing what you've already written. For example, when you write a blog post, consider using the idea, or even the word-for-word prose, in a video you can post anywhere from YouTube to Instagram. If you have a podcast, you can host a clip on your blog, in your newsletter, and social media, directing viewers to listen to the full episode on your podcast page. Pull any great tips or quotes from the episode for social media. If you've written one witty post for social media, created one stellar video, or poured your heart into a long newsletter, it would be a waste to send it out into the universe just once! In a busy, fast, and transient online universe, you can't afford to be shy, and you shouldn't worry about bothering your following—it's much more likely they didn't see it the first time.

Well-executed repurposing can look like:

You've now effectively hit five different potential audiences with one piece of content. And those who consume it across several formats are your most avid fans—the fans most likely to buy your book.

My client Dan Martell, whom you were introduced to in Step 1, did this well. What he seemed to know innately was that his audience of software entrepreneurs would come to his material in different ways; it would be a mistake to be present on just one medium to the exclusion of others. So he provided a YouTube channel where, if you are someone who spends free time looking at videos, you can find Dan talking in his singularly animated way. Or if you're an audible learner rather than a visual one, you can listen to his podcast. If you prefer short-form nuggets of wisdom, you can read Dan's blog posts. Your creation should have multimedia appeal because individuals consume ideas in all kinds of ways. Before they go to search for your book on Amazon, most have either toed the water or even steeped themselves in your work.

IF YOU PREFER TO ENGAGE OFFLINE

We've covered the three most effective ways to build an online presence—a website, an e-mail list, and social media. But there are other factors that are meaningful in our evaluation of platform and don't necessarily require you to be visible online. Non-tech people rejoice! The methods below are also proven to be effective at drawing an audience to your work.

Network

Think of networking as making meaningful and helpful connections with others in your field. If you're not inclined to reach out and make connections, I'm not here to force you to do it. But I'd like you to consider the value that agents and editors see in a network, especially for those who wish to steer clear of a public online profile. A network can be anything from the organizations that support or have hired you to the authors, journalists, and podcasters who know your name to the influencers in your field. Authors are generally collegial people. They can connect you with agents, promote your work, introduce you to their audience, endorse your book when it comes out, and generally support and advise you along the way. This makes a network a powerful asset that can impress a publisher and win you a book deal, no enormous online following required.

If you're starting with a network of zero substantial contacts and need to make those connections, you have to determine—and then persuade—those you begin to reach out to of the win-win. When James Clear was not yet a known name and planning the launch of *Atomic Habits*, he reached out to Susan Peirce Thompson and asked for her support. It's hard to imagine now, but back then, like most first-time authors, he needed all the help he could get. At the time, Susan recorded a weekly "vlog" (video blog) that was regularly watched by tens of thousands of people. Wanting to support James in a big way, she did a vlog about his book and told her audience that for anyone who purchased the book and sent her a receipt, she would send a link to an exclusive Zoom conversation she and James had together. Using this strategy, Susan's audience single-handedly accounted for 4,000 sales of *Atomic Habits* when it first launched. Though the book went on to be a juggernaut, those sales contributed to its rise in the bestseller lists in those crucial first weeks. While most people would have just included a link in their newsletter or sent out a tweet, Susan went above and beyond to create a unique offer that hugely benefited James and her own audience.

When Susan's own book, *Rezoom*, published a few years later, she asked James to provide an endorsement. While James receives countless requests for blurbs, he was happy to reciprocate the favor Susan had provided him when he was starting out. They had built a genuine relationship that began with mutual value. Don't overthink what this could be. Often just your time in the room with another author or sincerely and consistently promoting someone else's book will be perceived as a memorable gesture no matter how unknown you are.

If networking could be a strength in your platform, you'll want to showcase your genuine connections—your *real* relationships—not just a link to someone you exchanged a few lines with on X (formerly Twitter). Agents and editors will be wary if you claim to know Oprah or anticipate getting featured on her podcast. It's an amateur error that I don't want to see you make!

Bylines

Penning articles, essays, and op-eds can be an effective way to demonstrate a platform for any aspiring authors and specifically for narrative nonfiction writers, novelists, and memoirists. I'm considering bylines as an "offline" endeavor because historically, this referred to writing for print newspapers and magazines. These days, you would be hard-pressed to find an article or essay that isn't published online, but writing for these publications does not require you to be an online marketer, and that's the notable difference. Still, the benefits of a published piece often generate a ripple effect in an important *on*line way—multiplying your social media following by hundreds of strangers you would not have ordinarily reached. It's a hack writers are pleased to learn! You should view these published pieces as another way to establish your recognition as a writer or expert and attract attention to your work. Bylines also signal to agents and editors that you have connections in media, which is naturally advantageous when it comes to launching a book later.

Speaking

Giving regular talks is one of the most effective methods we see over and over again to sell books, and it applies in particular to business and personal development authors. Companies that you consult for or have relationships with are primed to buy multiple copies of your book when they host you for a speaking appearance. The second client I signed early in my career, right from out of the slush pile, was a regular speaker with connections to Goldman Sachs and American Express, among others. His consulting company was brand new and unknown, and in fact, he was soon headed to live overseas! This was going to be a challenge. But Rajeev developed a thoughtful and in-depth marketing plan that convinced me (and publishers) there was a strategy for earning back a publisher's investment. Simon & Schuster took a chance on him in a six-figure deal.

Fiction, narrative nonfiction, and memoir writers, you won't be evaluated for your speaking credentials, but it certainly won't be seen as a disadvantage! If you're a skilled and frequent public speaker who loves the spotlight, speaking can be a considerable asset to your platform—and something agents will care to learn.

Podcasts

It seems like everyone has a podcast these days. Do I need one? I'm glad to reassure you: you don't. The options above should give you manifold opportunities for growing a platform. But if you're drawn to the broadcast world, and you're ready to make the time investment, podcasting can be a great path for selling books and finding readers. Melissa Houston, a student of our Get Signed course, created the *She Means Profit* podcast well before she had a deal for her debut book, *Cash Confident*. As a CPA, Melissa loves helping women entrepreneurs master their finances. She decided the simplest and most enjoyable way for her to do this was through audio interviews, which allowed her to make connections with well-known personalities in her space. Within a couple of years, this grew into an impressive network of influencers and an engaged community of fans that proved to publishers that there was a foundation to support her book.

Building a podcast with enough downloads to attract an agent is a long game, like most platform-building. A shortcut is hitching onto the platform of others. Pitching yourself to appear on other podcasts that reach your intended crowd is a good way to reach more readers and build connections with the hosts.

Whichever medium attracts you enough to show up consistently for an audience, you will see results, little by little, as you keep building. Dorie Clark, in her book, coincidentally called *The Long Game*, refers to these as "raindrops." You'll feel only a few to begin, which will validate the work you're doing. Then suddenly, though it may take years, you'll see a downpour.

Now that we've covered your big idea, your market, your readership, your authority, and the platform that's going to let you show it all off, you have everything you need to start pitching agents. Things are about to get real! But before we get there, let's take a quick detour, where I'll reveal the Four Kinds of Writers Who Get Book Deals. It's one of my favorite things for aspiring authors to discover—the strengths that will serve you most in querying and beyond. These are the traits I have seen countless times in the most successful authors.

Let's find out what kind of writer you are.

INTERMISSION

The Four Kinds of Writers
Who Get Book Deals

I was eight weeks into my maternity leave, not looking to sign new clients, when one of my authors called. "My friend wants to book a flight to New York to meet with you. I completely understand if you need to say no. But trust me, it's worth a meeting."

Just one day later, Ron met me at a café a block from my apartment. After some small talk, he pulled a crisply printed collated document from his briefcase and put it in front of me. I couldn't help but laugh—presenting a book proposal this way was so old-school, it was charming. Ron was pitching a book that would shed light on the little-known practices used by the greatest craftspeople, athletes, chefs, and business leaders of all time. He called it *Unstoppable Momentum.*

An earlier version of Ron's proposal had already been submitted by a previous agent to several major publishers and was passed on, in several cases without so much as a response from editors. I knew that it would be an uphill battle to go back into the trenches with something the market had already seen.

But as I read Ron's proposal, I felt a tingling in my spine, the physical reaction I have when I discover a new talent with huge potential. The document was unputdownable—commercially savvy, rigorous in its research, engrossing in its writing. I also saw some important tweaks worth making. Like so many of my most ambitious and creative authors, Ron was packing too much into one book, and his proposal lacked the kind of singular focus that editors want to see. As executive editor Stephanie Frerich once described it to me, a proposal should clearly signal "the one thing you want someone to do, or to rethink, upon reading your book."

With this in mind, Ron and I took the three ideas initially presented in his proposal and distilled the concept into a single book about "decoding greatness" through the little-known art and science of reverse-engineering. By the time we submitted this fresh, novel concept, its singularity was so distinguished from his earlier, far denser document that editors viewed it as a completely new proposal—and it elicited multiple bids in a heated auction. Even the very editors who had initially passed participated!

Decoding Greatness sold to Simon & Schuster for six times the advance Ron received for a book he had sold at the beginning of his career called *The Best Place to Work*. And what Ron and I repackaged as book two from the ideas in his original proposal went to the same publisher for an even larger advance. What we effectively achieved was generating more than double the advance of one book by turning his initial proposal into a series.

So, how did Ron do it? How did he manage to convince me, and eventually a big-name publisher, to take a chance on him after he'd been turned down so many times? He played to his authorial strengths.

Writers win over agents for different reasons. It's reasonable to expect that there will be an area or two where your natural strengths shine brighter. Over time, I've noticed a set of traits that recur in authors, and they become immediately distinguishable in a first meeting or even a query letter. When I see those traits, I know I'm looking at an author capable of finding a buyer. These traits can be translated into four kinds of writers who get book deals.

The Ideator excels at Step 1: They think big picture and always have an idea on the tip of the tongue.

The Data Collector is an expert in Steps 2 and 3: They understand the market.

The Crusader has mastered Step 4: They own their authority.

The Everywhereist nails Step 5: They know how to get seen by building a platform.

As we walk through the four kinds of writers, consider this question: What are *your* natural skills and assets that will be attractive to agents and editors? Was there a step that appealed most to you?

In Ron's case, he was a pollster in a previous job, where it was his duty to collect data about public opinion. Later, after receiving a degree in social psychology, he noticed a burgeoning interest among corporations in his area of research and saw a different, more lucrative career ahead as a speaker and consultant. Many people need a book to do that successfully. There are numerous ways in which Ron shined as a prospective author, but he made his strongest case when he used his scientific skills to his advantage.

When I asked him, "What's your big idea? Why do you think people will buy this book?", he didn't hesitate. He had a research-backed and succinct answer for every question I posed. I came to find out that he had practiced them as well.

Even Ron's process for querying was data-driven. When he decided to pursue an agent, he gathered the names of the agents in the acknowledgments section of all of the books that inspired him and put them in a spreadsheet. Then he collected e-mail addresses. Some he couldn't find, so he began guessing at handles with first name, last initial, then last name, first initial, etc. He even used a website that can confirm whether an e-mail address is working or not. I cannot fully endorse this method, but it speaks to the drive and obsession that serves a Data Collector well. After confirming the agents' e-mail addresses, he researched to see what other authors those agents represented. He made a point to mention them in his query letter.

But Ron isn't just a Data Collector; he's an Ideator. Ron has a good idea at least once a week, a great idea every month, and a groundbreaking idea at least six times a year. He even admitted to me that he also has a complete 70,000-word novel tucked away somewhere on his computer. I wonder how much we can sell that one for!

Much like Ron, you'll find how your writer type can guide you to a positive outcome. It's actually more than likely you will identify with at least two types. And based on what you've read thus far, you have the information and hopefully the confidence to strengthen the areas where you may be weaker. Let's take a closer look at the four types.

THE IDEATOR

The Ideator gets a book deal by demonstrating a really powerful idea. They convince publishers that they can sell books by positioning their book as a true game changer— an idea that's so compelling, it will be irresistible to the media and readers.

The natural energy of Ideators becomes readily apparent to a publisher. The best way we can work with them as agents is by harnessing that energy and reining in the various pieces to fit under one umbrella topic, much like Ron and I did together. As you now know, there can be a hundred hooks, but a big idea stands alone. Ideators are collaborative and can pivot quickly, given a new trend in the marketplace or an agent's feedback. Because their ideas are prolific and novel, they also signal to agents and publishers that they have versatility and a greater career beyond one book—a huge asset.

Ideators often hold positions where their creativity can shine. Most commonly, they are entrepreneurs. If you have a notebook full of ideas with little time to execute them all, you might be an Ideator.

THE DATA COLLECTOR

The Data Collector gets a book deal by demonstrating the success of similar books. They do their homework and convince industry insiders that they have the ability to sell books based on their research of what has worked before and what readers are looking for now. Ron had a shelf full of similar books from which he did his agent research and had studied Amazon extensively. The same reverse engineering e-mail address skills aided him in Amazon deep dives to discover what people were reading and how his book filled a gap in the marketplace.

Data Collectors tend to be scientists, academics, journalists, or novelists. They are often introverts first and foremost, more comfortable with back-end research than self-promotion. Crystal clear on where their books fall in the market, they are masters of positioning.

THE CRUSADER

The Crusader gets a book deal by demonstrating unrelenting commitment and resourcefulness. They convince agents and publishers they have the ability to sell books by openly pursuing their publishing goals with fervor. Ultimately, they will not stop until they convince you of their merit, talent, and inevitable success. This changes the question in an agent's mind from *Does this person have what it takes?* to *Do I want this person to succeed with me or someone else?*

For many writers, getting an agent to say yes is one of the hardest, most anxiety-provoking pieces of the process. But the Crusader lives for the close. Competitive and aggressive by nature, the Crusader gets increasingly motivated by rejection, determined to find their way in. Crusaders never see the door as shut. They just keep coming back with ideas.

The tenacious Crusader self-advocates fearlessly and does a few other things well too. They are always on the hunt for a new agent to add to their query list until they land one. They find the right, significant update to follow up with if they receive no response—a tactic I'm excited to show you later. Publishers recognize immediately that a Crusader is a fantastic promoter for their mission. As a famous author I worked with, who I'll leave nameless here, put it: "My goal with this book is world domination."

Crusaders are often CEOs, entrepreneurs, marketers, salespeople, publicists, or producers. The Crusader/Ideator or the Crusader/Everywhereist are combination types I encounter regularly, and they're some of my most inspiring clients. If one of your greatest attributes is your tenacity, you could be a Crusader, and every genre of writer can use this natural ability to their advantage.

THE EVERYWHEREIST

The fourth kind of writer is what I call the Everywhereist—the writer who is highly visible and has a platform. The Everywhereist is the writer type that every publisher is seeking, so if you bring this to the table, agents are ready to hear from you. Immediately. The Everywhereist gets a book deal by demonstrating their audience and reach. Their Google results are pages deep.

The Everywhereist recognizes that captivating an audience of people who are enthusiastic about your ideas is the order of the day, and visibility is simply an ally (much like Colette Baron-Reid said of Motörhead). Many of our authors at Lucinda Literary are Everywhereists. Dr. Mary Barbera comes to mind because long before she was able to secure media coverage, which happened during her book launch, her website and courses about parenting children with autism came up in Google's first pages of search results, including courses, customer reviews, and various other mentions—a classic Everywhereist.

Having published her first book with a very small press and receiving no advance, Mary was incredulous when I called to let her know that we'd secured a major deal with her dream publisher. The Everywhereist leads their pitch with the confidence of their audience behind them.

Everywhereists can be influencers, bloggers, and content mavens. They are prolific creators who are sometimes big personalities unafraid to practice in public. They tend to have a wide network, and as their material gets noticed, it generates meaningful connections in their industry. Everywhereists often begin as Data Collectors in marketing before they foray into building their platform. The Everywhereist/Data Collector combination is one I find magnetic.

If you're someone with a track record of sharing your story and getting traction from it in some way, you could be an Everywhereist.

WHAT'S MY TYPE?

Select just one answer for each question below. Then turn the page to discover which writer type you most resemble!

What part of developing your book do you most enjoy?

- a. Researching material to include in the book
- b. Talking to my network about my book ideas
- c. The inspiration and connection I get from collaborating with others on my work
- d. Brainstorming new ideas

I am most comfortable:

- a. When I have done my research and am totally prepared
- b. Winging it on a big stage
- c. Using the Internet to share my content
- d. Writing articles with new, groundbreaking content

I think of myself as:

- a. A strong listener and observer
- b. A big personality and voice
- c. Happiest when I'm connecting with others, preferably from my phone
- d. Happiest when I'm in a room by myself being creative

I struggle with:

    a.   A fear of the unknown

    b.   Patience

    c.   Being alone or disconnected from others

    d.   Grounding my dreams in reality

Agents will find my work:

    a.   Well-argued, clearly executed, and credible

    b.   Provocative and bold

    c.   Appealing and helpful to a wide readership

    d.   Exciting and original

Agents will enjoy working with me because:

    a.   I take feedback seriously

    b.   I never shy away from calling in favors

    c.   I am a born public promoter

    d.   I'm always dreaming up new stories

Two characteristics that best describe me are:

    a.   Rational and curious

    b.   Resourceful and tenacious

    c.   Influential and collaborative

    d.   Creative and adaptable

Answer Key

Mostly A's = Data Collector   *Mostly B's = Crusader*

Mostly C's = Everywhereist   *Mostly D's = Ideator*

Now I'm going to teach you how to write a query letter according to your strengths, whichever writer type you are. You'll discover that there are nonnegotiable, crucial elements you must get right. But it's also an art as much as it is science to piece it together, and I'll give you a formula to follow.

It's time to pitch.

STEP 6

Pitch
Persuasively

Dear Lucinda,
I sent out my query letter to dozens of agents months
ago and never heard back from any of them.
What am I doing wrong?

— KATIE (CHICAGO, IL)

We have arrived at the step where I dish everything you need to know about the query letter, a memo of 300 words or less that you will send to agents to solicit interest in your work. The previous five steps have all been leading you here, where we put everything together, highlight your strengths, strategize the execution, and refine it more times than you might expect. A great pitch makes Alex Littlefield, an executive editor at Little, Brown, an imprint of Hachette, "forget all the other reservations" he might have. It has the ethereal quality of something we have been looking for all along but didn't know until we saw it. A pitch can be, in other words, a dealmaker. Your movie trailer. Most of us have come to expect more than a book from a book. We're visualizing it on the screen.

In the olden days, writers would send their query letters by snail mail with a big, heavy manuscript. Now they are received entirely by e-mail. *Easier!* it would be logical to think. But actually it's the reverse. At least someone would open the envelope to see what was inside. Today, a poorly executed e-mail does not require anyone to open it at all.

FORGET EVERYTHING YOU'VE HEARD

Can I ask you to do something wild? Scrap everything you know about query letters as you enter this chapter, even if you're a seasoned querier. If you're entirely new to the process, all the better—I won't have to undo any outdated advice.

Your book could be the accumulation of 20 years' experience in your field, the bravest thing you've ever done, your life's story, your *magnum opus*. But here's the thing: if you love your book, you're going to have to let it go—for the moment. Leave your writer hat at the door and, as Ariel Lawhon says, put on your "author hat." The one that gets you a deal. You can be a writer no matter how your book enters the world, but traditional publishing is a business first. And you have to know the rules of that business to succeed.

First, here are some rules that you definitely don't want to follow. These are just a few myths circulating online:

Agents don't care who you are, so you shouldn't include any information about yourself in your letter.

I hope I've now proved that this is entirely untrue. Whether it's your bylines, your e-mail list, the author friends who will endorse your work, or an immediate grasp of your voice, we want a sense of why readers will trust you as their guide through whatever territory they're exploring.

A long and detailed synopsis should be the focus of your letter.

While other agencies may wish for this, use the model of the Amazon description to capture your book's greatest intrigue or payoff, not the traditional synopses you learned in writing or literature class.

You shouldn't include identifying information about your book, like title or genre, if you're at all unsure.

As we talked about in Step 2, take your best guess and customize to the person receiving your note.

Never contact an agent directly unless their submissions page says so.

In a moment, I'll reveal that whatever you're told, finding a direct e-mail to an agent is a more effective route to ensure your query actually gets a look.

Don't follow up. An agent will always reach out to you if interested.

One can hope! But hope isn't a strategy. Agents may only see your query the second time, especially if you can entice them with an update.

Reach out to every agent possible at once.

There are several risks to this, and one is that a slush approach is unlikely to appear as anything *but* slush. Agents are flattered—and can tell—when they're part of a small and curated list.

You only get one shot.

Is a door really ever closed? Maybe you're asking the wrong person (I'm a Crusader). Whether submitting a revision of your material or something new all together, plenty of writers—including several I've signed—find success the second time around.

Brevity First

Those in the news industry have been known to say that the headline is more important than the article, because if you can't get someone to read the article, who cares what you've written? Similarly, if you can't get someone to read your book, you've already lost the battle.

When the pitch for *Tangerine*, by Christine Mangan, crossed her desk, Elisabeth Weed, a partner at the Book Group—representing some of the biggest names in fiction—instantly saw cinematic appeal. The novel, set in Tangier, Morocco, in the 1960s, is about two women who fall in love but, as the query letter suggested, with a *Talented Mr. Ripley*-esque twist. Between the exotic setting, the unconventional characters, and the suggestion of suspense, Elisabeth knew she had a smash hit on her hands. *Tangerine*'s film rights were later optioned to George Clooney with Scarlett Johansson to star.

A common misconception is that a query letter should be a synopsis of your book. I understand why it seems logical—at first. But unless an agency's guidelines require it, I wouldn't even lead your letter with a synopsis, just as you wouldn't want to lead with a title you're fairly sure is a goner. The key is to lead *only* with your strengths. Lettered credentials? Recognized bylines? Awards? An e-mail list into the thousands? Killer comps? This is where you might start, intriguing us in the very first paragraph.

For many agents, your synopsis is secondary. If intrigued enough to begin reading, we'll either be quickly rooted in the characters and plot, or we won't. Agents, editors, and readers care first about the elements that make your book or your career promising. Less is more. Stripping down a lengthy synopsis to its key elements is a far safer bet than sharing information beyond the scope of what we care to learn. Don't worry, I'll ask you if I want more details!

What do I mean by "key elements"? For novels and memoirs, a synopsis should include the main characters—only the main characters—and an idea of where the story starts and finishes. This should give us a sense of the stakes, which should be high. Do not neglect the pivotal moment, or climax, that readers will experience. A story should have a beginning, middle, and end. Agents need to glimpse the arc from a bird's-eye view. What we don't want? Anything that reads like a laundry list.

For narrative or research-based titles, the critical elements are "newsbreaks," information not yet disclosed in the public domain. For practical nonfiction, we're looking for concrete takeaways. *Surprising* and *counterintuitive* are our favorite words. You might consider nixing any takeaway or plot point that can't be described this way. If you focus on surprise, you avoid a common pitfall: sounding generic.

For all genres, think memorable and relatable. If you are writing science fiction, for example, a strong description will contain a character, sentiment, or atmosphere that feels familiar to you, but the adventure you're taking us on will feel instantly exciting. In nonfiction, the book's core thesis or takeaway should make an immediate impression, lingering with the person who is searching for the next great read on the topic. For agents and editors, it's very personal. As Sarah Pelz, an executive editor at HarperCollins, told me, "I look for things that relate to my interests. All of my books are connected to my life in some way."

Isn't that like all of us—editors, agents, and readers? You want to break through to people, to let their mind percolate on the incredible things they're about to learn that they've never heard before—at least not in quite the same way as you will be recounting them. Aim for unforgettable; settle for desirable.

You can let the reader guide the way in your query. By now you know well who your reader is. But if you want your book in the world, you will need to know how to talk about it.

THE MOST POWERFUL SENTENCES IN YOUR PITCH

I have an experiment for you. Tell me what your book is about in a couple lines, as if you had just met me in an elevator and you only had a minute to spare. This, of course, is the origin of the term "elevator pitch." Your elevator pitch is 1,000 percent more important than the long synopsis I told you to chuck a moment ago. You'll need to recite it in meetings with agents and publishers; you'll need it for your NPR interview. And it's a major factor in your query letter too.

Try to get that elevator pitch right in the first paragraph of your query letter, and go ahead and bold it if you think it's especially attention-grabbing (noting that every elevator pitch should be). While you may not know it, the elevator pitch is present on every book retailer's page. It was probably what compelled you to buy your last purchase on Amazon. Or your last anything. It's the sneaky device that just kicked a standard book description up about 10 levels. You can use this device to a winning advantage in your query letter—no matter what an agency's guidelines tell you. That's right: I'm giving you permission to break the rules. As Peter Heller confided when I interviewed him: "To be honest, Lucinda, I never obeyed any of those rules."

Strict guidelines can dampen your creativity and dim your star potential. So even if you're asked to include only a synopsis, find a way to remodel it with a stunning elevator pitch. Why not follow the current method that works with actual book buyers? If an agency is looking at the next Stephen King, will they take you to task for not giving the exact word count they originally requested? Please!

Here's how the elevator pitch fits into the Amazon description for Marie Kondo's blockbuster bestseller *The Life-Changing Magic of Tidying Up.*

> *Despite constant efforts to declutter your home, do papers still accumulate like snowdrifts and clothes pile up like a tangled mess of noodles?*
>
> *Japanese cleaning consultant Marie Kondo takes tidying to a whole new level, promising that if you properly simplify and organize your home once, you'll never have to do it again. Most methods advocate a room-by-room or little-by-little approach, which doom you to pick away at your piles of stuff forever. The KonMari Method, with its revolutionary category-by-category system, leads to lasting results. In fact, none of Kondo's clients have lapsed (and she still has a three-month waiting list).*
>
> *With detailed guidance for determining which items in your house "spark joy" (and which don't), this international bestseller will help you clear your clutter and enjoy the unique magic of a tidy home—and the calm, motivated mindset it can inspire.*

The elevator pitch is essentially the first sentence combined with the last: *"Japanese cleaning consultant Marie Kondo takes tidying to a whole new level, promising that if you properly simplify and organize your home once, you'll never have to do it again. With detailed guidance for determining which items in your house 'spark joy' (and which don't), this international bestseller will help you clear your clutter and enjoy the unique magic of a tidy home—and the calm, motivated mindset it can inspire."*

The whole description is well done, but what stands out most in the elevator pitch are the two now-famous words: *spark joy*. The more distilled you can make what executive editor at Viking Rick Kot calls a "payoff" for the reader, the better. Try to include just one, two, or three words that capture the promise of your book. I know—it's hard! I opened by giving you one minute to pitch and now I'm asking you to distill, distill, distill until your entire concept has been whittled down to a few key sentences. Agents look for the quick, catchy, indelible phrase that a reader can't forget.

For a fiction example, here is the Amazon description for Judy Lin's novel *A Magic Steeped in Poison*:

> *I used to look at my hands with pride. Now all I can think is, "These are the hands that buried my mother."*
>
> *For Ning, the only thing worse than losing her mother is knowing that it's her own fault. She was the one who unknowingly brewed the poison tea that killed her—the poison tea that now threatens to also take her sister, Shu.*
>
> *When Ning hears of a competition to find the kingdom's greatest shennong-shi—masters of the ancient and magical art of tea-making—she travels to the imperial city to compete. The winner will receive a favor from the princess, which may be Ning's only chance to save her sister's life.*
>
> *But between the backstabbing competitors, bloody court politics, and a mysterious (and handsome) boy with a shocking secret, Ning might actually be the one in more danger.*

The problem for the main character is clearly introduced from the first few lines. There is excitement, stakes, world building, adventure, and the tease of something even more exciting in just three short paragraphs. The aesthetics are also immediately apparent (ancient and magical art, imperial city, princess, court politics), transporting any reader instantaneously.

TRY IT: MASTER YOUR ELEVATOR PITCH

Remember the speed-pitch exercise we rehearsed in Step 1? Use every meeting, every cocktail party, every conversation as an opportunity to speed pitch, refining those crucial two lines that will showcase your book's potential. In doing so, you may find there are also ways you can be simplifying and improving the very proposal or manuscript you're pitching. Here are a few questions to reflect on after you've practiced your pitch.

For fiction authors:

- Was it difficult to nail down the inciting incident, or did it take too long to get there? (This is a key way to diagnose if your book needs to be more tightly structured and fast-paced.)

- Did it feel impossible to discuss the arcs of just one or two characters?

- Did you feel the need to babble about a dozen plot points? This might be a sign that you need to narrow the focus, no matter how narratively complex it may be on the page.

For nonfiction authors:

- Did you address the critical "why this book now?"

- Did you struggle to distill your main takeaway for the reader into a sentence?

- Did you include any credentials that would make you an author to trust?

For both:

- Can you pitch your book in under a minute?
- Did your tongue trip over your title and subtitle?
- Was there an element of surprise?
- Does it have cadence and rhythm? Meaning, does it sound natural and smooth when you speak it?

When you try your elevator pitch on friends, watch for facial movement. That's a good sign they're intrigued (unless you're receiving an outright frown!). Do they appear confused and compelled to ask a clarifying question? The way you say your pitch out loud is how agents and publishers will hear it in their heads.

You can even engage an artificial intelligence device to see what it thinks of your elevator pitch. One of the best uses of AI platforms for artists and marketers of all kinds is as a sounding board for short pitches. While AI tools will not be able to replicate your voice or what is unique about your profile, it *can* offer alternate wording and ways to tighten your pitch. Who knows, you may end up liking ChatGPT's suggestions more than your own!

After you've improved your verbal pitch to the best of your abilities, e-mail it to a friend whose taste you admire and will give it to you straight. Write, revise, pitch, and revise again—your pitch and your material can work hand in hand. Take the time to get this right. An elevator pitch you can write with confidence is vital to your query letter.

THE TWO RULES OF A GREAT QUERY LETTER

When I went looking for typical guidelines of what fellow agencies are looking for in a query letter, I stumbled upon requirements like a "sales handle," "logline," "positioning memo," "marketing information," and "a description of the author's biography."

You may already be familiar with this terminology or recognize some of these phrases from the previous steps, but still, do we need to be so corporate about it all? Writing is a craft—shouldn't the way you present yourself to agents communicate personality, originality, and flare? More than a "sales handle" or a "sale history," here's what really sells: a good story. All you need to do is convince an agent that you have one.

Here are two simple rules to query by.

Rule #1: Open with your strengths.

Hook the reader in your very first sentence. Contrary to everything I learned in school, I like to keep the opening to every e-mail I send to one line, two at most. Every e-mail should be designed to ease the weary eye. That first and second line should grab an agent's attention immediately. Usually, it will be a combination of the elevator pitch and your book's greatest asset. Sometimes *you* are the asset. These sentences vary from writer to writer depending on what you personally bring to the table. If you are an Everywhereist with impressive social media numbers, start there. If you are a Data Collector and have a standout comp or statistic about your genre, put it front and center. Ideators should get right to the book's takeaways because they're that one-of-a-kind. Crusaders might lead with the credibility they have built or charm us with a witty introduction. All of these hooks are effective, and we'll discuss several ways to implement them.

Rule #2: Close with a call to action.

I'm all for kindness and consideration, but many authors are overanxious about sounding pushy or being a "bother." Remember that many agents will not even see your query letter the first time. There is virtually no such thing as being too aggressive or urgent in your closing—because agents tend to be aggressive and urgent people. We get it! I was long ago taught that the unspecific "let me know" is never the most effective way to end an e-mail. (Don't worry, I'm about to give you some better alternatives.)

The closing of your letter is your last chance to capture an agent's interest, so get the clock ticking. If you have any competitive interest in your book, share this. Or disclose that you've had multiple requests for material, or that the agent you're querying is on a small list of those you are considering, or that publishers have already requested your proposal—use anything you've got. If someone notable has endorsed, edited, or stands behind your project, say so. You might choose comps to show that there's an appetite for your work, latch on to a topic that's trending, or find another way to express your book's timeliness. If you don't have any of these things, heart, motivation, and personality (like your willingness to collaborate) can go a long way.

Here are closing lines that would get my attention:

- "Thank you for your consideration. For full transparency, I have had several agents request my manuscript, but I am most interested in your representation. I look forward to hearing from you soon."

- "Thank you for your time. The [topic requires] that people take action immediately or this problem will only get worse. I hope to hear from you about the full proposal soon, given the timeliness of this issue."

- "My manuscript is complete at 97,000 words, and Colleen Hoover, with whom I have a direct connection, has promised to write a glowing blurb about it. Would you like to see the full manuscript?"

- "With thousands of followers across all channels, my social media presence is intrinsically tied to this project, and I expect that a high percentage of my followers would convert to readers. My book proposal is available upon your request."

- "I'm in the process of interviewing agents and looking to make a decision in the next two weeks. I would be honored for your consideration of my brief proposal."

The strongest closing lines are those that force a dialogue by raising a question or requesting a specific action. These are harder to ignore and more likely to yield a reply.

THE ANATOMY OF A QUERY LETTER

With the two rules in mind, here is the breakdown of what we want to see in your letter. These are guidelines only, but they attempt to universalize what every agent wants to see. Include them all if you can.

- Subject line: _____
  (if agency submission form allows)
- Personal introduction
- Title
- Genre
- Elevator pitch
- Credentials or platform, if any
- Comps
- Differentiation (the "wow" factor)
- Call to action

We've talked about most of these ingredients in the previous sections of this book, but we haven't yet covered the first two: the subject line and the introduction.

Subject Lines

For me, the subject line is the deciding factor in whether I open a pitch immediately, let it linger, or ignore it completely. Many agencies have submission portals and formal guidelines, requiring that writers submit in a particular way, but if you can find a direct e-mail to an agent—and mostly all are available through Publishers Marketplace—you are best positioned to make a connection. And if you can land on a subject line for your e-mail that intrigues immediately, then it's far more likely that an agent will *open* your e-mail. As I said before, we definitely don't want to miss the next Stephen King. We're not going to fault you for your poor manners—if we're interested. The first achievement is this: you got opened!

Let's look at some winning examples of subject lines:

- *Licensed Psychologist and Speaker on Why We Should Give Up on "Happiness"*

- *Commercial Fiction Query for Women Who Cheat: Sophie Kinsella Meets Emily Henry*

- *For admirers of Susan Cain and Dan Pink: What The 48 Laws of Power Got Wrong*

- *Congratulations on your recent deal for [BOOK TITLE]: a submission of interest to you?*

- *Time-sensitive submission for literary novel [BOOK TITLE]*

- *First book by journalist for The Washington Post: newsbreaking biography of [PERSON]*

- *Debut YA Novel from #OwnVoices Author & Contributor to NYT Modern Love Column*

- *The Taste Bud's Adventure: SCBWI Member's Latest Children's Book*

- *You Could Be Having Better Sex book proposal by Ph.D. and UW's most popular "sex" professor*

- *The Simple Path to Wealth for Millennials*

If your book title is hands down phenomenal, your subject line can be as simple as that. Titles like *They Both Die at the End* or *I'm Glad My Mom Died* would have grabbed me like a news headline that I could not miss! Tabitha Carvan, despite zero social media presence, received a deal for *This Is Not a Book About Benedict Cumberbatch*. The title's bold statement and invitation to learn more did a lot of the leg work for her. (Further, as you'll also see in a query letter example that follows, when you don't have a fan base yourself, you can leverage the fan base of the subject you're exploring.)

If you're unsure about your book title itself but are seeking new representation, have an offer, or were referred by a mutual connection, these are all options for enhancing your subject line.

Subject lines are another great place to make use of artificial intelligence tools like ChatGPT. If you're stuck on what to put in the blank, simply enter a brief synopsis and ask an AI engine what it would use as a subject line for an e-mail. You may not want to use exactly what it recommends, but it can be a helpful place to start if you need creative ideas.

Personal Introduction

You wouldn't believe how many writers pitch agents by the wrong name, entirely confuse them with a different agent they had in mind, or worst of all, slush 20 or more agents with one e-mail! Most have not researched the actual genres the agent represents, and this reeks of desperation. If your letter feels like an obvious template or form letter, you have already negatively impacted someone's first impression. The best letters, in my view, feel as though a peer is contacting you in a conversational manner. Or as Penguin Random House executive editor Paul Whitlatch puts it, "Have the sensibility of the author's voice."

When you write to someone you don't know and request their time and attention, you want to create a win-win, or suggest a mutual benefit. Just as in a cover letter for a job application, if someone's personal passions are made clear but the value they would provide is left unclear, the applicant has missed the mark.

To really prove the win-win to the agent, do your research on the agent/agency you're submitting to and *always* insert a line or two in your letter about why you're approaching that agent specifically. This is commonly the opening line to your query letter, and when you really want someone, it can often feature in the close. Agents will take notice when you reference recent sales or clients on their list as influences (because flattery always wins); you are priming them to spend a little extra time and attention when considering your pitch and material.

David Halpern, vice president at the Robbins Office literary agency, says he reads every pitch from his slush pile that opens with a personal introduction and genuinely shows the writer has read at least one of his authors. "Mystery-thriller writer Katie Tallo queried me as a huge Peter Heller fan, and it was evident from her note (and then our eventual conversations) that she was targeting possible representation based on the work she loved to read and with which she felt a real connection," David told me. "Even though she was not referred by a client, I called in her novel, which I loved." While not a guarantee, sending a thoughtful, personal letter immediately increases your chances of receiving a thoughtful, personal response.

Last point: whether the person you admire is "officially" taking on new talent or not, it can be difficult for an agent to ignore the temptation of a brilliant discovery, and there may be another agent we would be happy to send you to if we think the concept is commercial but not for us.

Tiny Tricks

You want to optimize your letter by keeping it concise while packing a lot of punch. Here are four easy ways to do that.

1. Link to an article, an interview, or a brief video clip as an excellent snapshot of what your book offers or to demonstrate credibility.

2. Include a bio under the signature line, especially if there are lots of points on your résumé. This breaks up the longer read, creating a cleaner format that keeps the eye moving.

3. Include sales or positive media response if you have successfully launched a business, product, or book previously.

4. If you have a great *brief* video clip—or better, a TED-like talk—include it prominently in your letter.

Sample Query Letters

The best way to determine a good query letter is to look at examples. For reference, I've compiled real query letters that caught an agent's attention and ignited a conversation. Though each one won't map perfectly onto your situation and idea, study them and learn from them. There are valuable lessons to be gained from each.

Notice how these letters follow the two rules and include the necessary parts of a successful pitch. Although they are organized differently, they strategically fit with the genre and target audience of the author. Use them as inspiration to get creative about how you want to write your own query.

SELF-DEVELOPMENT/HUMOR

Dear Agent,

I'm contacting you after coming across your profile and realizing that you agented [Book Title], a book that has greatly influenced my work, as well as [Book Title], one of my favorite reads in recent years. My name is Catherine Baab-Muguira, and I'm a writer who's contributed to *New York Magazine's* "The Cut," Playboy.com, Salon.com and FastCompany.com, among others. My June 2016 Quartz essay, "Millennials Are Obsessed with Side Hustles Because They're All We've Got," has been shared on Facebook more than 50,000 times and also became the focus of an April 2017 episode of NPR's On Point. I've just finished a nonfiction book proposal that I believe may be right up your alley—one that comes with some nice proof of concept, too.

In September of 2017, my essay, "Edgar Allan Poe Was a Broke-Ass Freelancer," ran on The Millions. It quickly became one of the site's most popular articles of the entire year and was picked up and shared by blogs and magazines including *Publishers Weekly* and *Arts & Letters Daily.*

But that piece was just a small excerpt from a much larger project I've been working on. It's called *How to Say "Nevermore" to Your Problems: Surprisingly Great Life Advice from Edgar Allan Poe, the World's Most Miserable Writer.* To put it glibly, it's the world's first ever self-help book based on Poe. It's one part Alain de Botton's *How Proust Can Change Your Life,* one part Jen Sincero's *You Are a Badass.*

Poe fans are legion: He has four million fans on Facebook alone, and there are Poe museums in New York, Philadelphia, Baltimore, and Richmond,

Virginia. Demand for works of Poe biography and criticism has stayed strong for nearly 200 years. And yet, while so much ink has been spilled, no one has ever looked to Poe for advice on how to live a fulfilling, worthy life.

I hope you'll like the voice and the direction I've taken with this premise, so I'm attaching my proposal and first chapter. If you'd like to discuss them, you can reach me by e-mail at [e-mail address] or at [phone number]. Thank you for your time and consideration.

All best,

Cat[5]

Dear Lucinda:

I'm the founder of dClutterfly, one of the nation's top de-cluttering businesses. We've received the "Super Service" award from Angie's List for the past five years, as well as have been lauded by Daily Candy as "Best in Nest." I've also been featured in magazines including *Fast Company* and on morning television talk shows. I'm contacting you because I'm working on my first book, which seemed like a smart fit for your list.

We're at a special moment in the de-cluttering sector. It's not that it's new; experts like Peter Walsh and even Julie Morgenstern have been penning bestsellers about tidying for decades. But what is new is the level of hunger for it—and the need. Marie Kondo, whose books include the #1 *New York Times* bestseller *The Life-Changing Magic of Tidying Up* and *Spark Joy*, is the latest bona fide craze. Why the craze? One reason being that even though American family size is shrinking, American consumption is growing exponentially (one study showed that 75% of families now use their garages as storage units, and storage itself is a $22 billion business annually). Another reason is the fact that we have 3% of the world's children but buy 40% of the world's toys . . . the list of reasons goes on.

I believe I have a unique perspective and patented method that can make my work that book for tidying. I am an American woman who has worked with over 1,000 clients (both Walsh and Kondo are foreigners, Australian and Japanese, respectively.) I have a personal relationship to clutter; my father was a hoarder, and many relatives grapple with garden-variety versions of the issue. As such, I look at de-cluttering through a more emotional, spiritual, and permanently helpful lens, as well as am a black belt in the physical elements of tidying. Many of my clients, in fact, have employed Kondo's "KonMari" method, but need something more fundamental to solve their problem. I'd like to share my approach with the millions of Americans looking for a lasting way out of the clutter trap.

I've put together an extensive outline and two sample chapters. May I send them along? As this query is out with just a small list of agents who I think will connect strongly with the material, I hope to discuss possibilities soon.

Best,
Tracy McCubbin

BUSINESS

Dear Lucinda,

I'm very excited to share the attached proposal for a business/ideas book called *Talent Nation: How to Be Part of the 10x Revolution*. My co-author Rishon Blumberg and I are the founders of 10x Management, a talent agency that began by representing rock stars like John Mayer and Vanessa Carlton and today represents the rock stars of the coding world. These coders deliver results that are above and beyond an average person's. From our unique perch as liaisons between today's top tech specialists and the companies that desperately need them, *Talent Nation* is our report from the front lines. It promises to empower not only the individual talent but the modern manager tasked with overseeing that individual's distinctive needs. And our approach can be applied to anyone in any industry.

Talent Nation posits that in today's new and ever-evolving work terrain, everyone needs to be both talent and management at once. They need to switch hats on a dime. This requires a new skill set no one is currently talking about, involving "skin in the game," an increased reliance on a third party, and the ability to spot the success and sabotage instincts, all of which we will illustrate through colorful real-world stories and interviews. Among the secrets we reveal, perhaps the greatest secret is this: those who constantly and openly seek feedback, and grow from it, will be at the helm of our increasingly automated world.

The talent economy is upon us with talent at the wheel, and those companies that have adapted their hiring and managing processes are succeeding precisely because they understand that this rare resource must be handled in a radically new way. As we argue, when tech is at the heartbeat of every venture, anyone who works for you can't simply be good—they must be great.

We've already heard strong interest in the proposal out of the gate from other agents and publishers. We hope we will have the opportunity to meet with you as well.

Thanks,
Michael Solomon

MEMOIR

Dear Lucinda,

I'm so grateful to be joining you for your Mastermind for Writers. My name is Devan Sandiford, and I'm bringing to the space my heart, my curiosity, and my book—*THE SILENCE WE CARRY: CONFESSIONS OF THE SIX-YEAR-OLD FATHER,* a memoir about how I suppressed the sorrow of a traumatic event in my childhood, hoping my silence would protect my family's peace. Think *Between the World and Me* meets *Mister Roger's Neighborhood.*

When I was six years old, my Uncle Ron was shot and killed by the police steps outside of my family's home. Faced with my mom's silence about her brother's death, I absorbed the belief that the best way to deal with pain was to keep it hidden inside. For twenty-eight years, that's exactly what I did. Then as a thirty-four-year-old father, I faced the truth that I was hurting my seven and four-year-old sons by burdening them with the weight of our family silence, forcing them to face hardships of racism and grief alone, and taking away their agency to make a change in the world.

Determined to provide a space for others who have endured similar histories, I started sharing the painful moments from my life on stages in New York City, Connecticut, Massachusetts, Toronto, and virtually all over the world. Over a two-year period, I shared more than fifty personal stories with crowds of as many as 1,200 people. One of my stories aired on a podcast alongside a story told by Rev. Al Sharpton, which led to it being downloaded over 1.2 million times and in 49 different countries. But even having witnessed my story resonate with so many people, it would take repeatedly seeing my sons carry the burden of my silence, and the murder of George Floyd, before I admitted to my mom that I wasn't the forever happy and peaceful man I had tried to be for her, but a confused six-year-old boy crushed by a lifetime of unspoken grief.

Although I am Black, my memoir is not about the police, racism, or the story of Black Lives Matter we hear on the news. It is a book about finding the courage to dance with the skeletons in our closets so we can grasp the connections we desperately need and reclaim the fullness of our humanity. It is an implicit call for everyone to talk about the silence we all carry—with our children, our parents, and anyone who has the courage to meet us in brave and vulnerable spaces.

Please note: I do have representation for my book through [LITERARY AGENCY], but I'm also thrilled that you create spaces where writers can receive feedback directly from agents, editors, and publishing insiders. It's with this intention that I'm sharing 9 pages of sample materials—as an introduction to my story and reference for your invaluable and highly recommended Lucinda Literary Mastermind for Writers.

With all my gratitude and excitement,

Devan Sandiford

FICTION

Dear Mr. Eck,

I'm pleased to share *The Replicant Prince*, a YA fantasy novel at 67,000 words envisioned as *Legendborn* meets *An Ember in the Ashes* and which has garnered interest from four publishers including Tor (Macmillan).

On a Mesopotamian-like planet called Paradise where cloning—once possible—is now outlawed, affable sixteen-year-old Taj survives an ambush and loses his memory. Two teens claiming to be his little sister and best friend swear he's the Prince of Paradise. But when another boy, who looks just like him, goes on television professing to be the real prince, Taj isn't sure what to believe. The trio journey through the harrowing Badlands—fending off deadly creatures, a murderous clan, and sandstorms—to locate a professor of genetics. Crippled by his faulty memories, Taj races against time, death, and an invisible enemy to uncover the truth. Is he the prince or is he the replicant?

I'm the author of The Colors Trilogy, a contemporary new adult series that sold more than 25,000 copies under my J-pad Publishing imprint. Each novel was a finalist in competitions (Foreword Reviews, National Indie Excellence) and garnered glowing reviews from

USA Today. I'm a member of Maryland Writers Association, Black Writers Guild, and IBPA. Utilizing my MBA, BS in engineering, and career in marketing, I know what it takes to get books in the hands of readers.

Below, I've included the first 10 pages of *The Replicant Prince*, professionally edited by Angela Brown, former editor in chief of Alyson Books.

Thank you for your time and consideration—I welcome the opportunity to connect further with you on potential representation for my newest work.

Sincerely,
K. R. Raye

FICTION

Dear Lucinda,

I came across your agency upon seeing *Fosse* by Sam Wasson, whose brilliant work I've followed for some time, on your website. I'm pleased and honored to submit to you my debut, *Price to Pay*, a thriller totaling 75,000 words in its completion. While I've had a number of short stories featured in *Bellevue Literary Review* and several nonfiction articles appear in the *Raritan* quarterly review, I believe this full-length, cinematic narrative has the trade potential a respected agency and traditional publisher might wish to consider.

In *Price to Pay*, Clive is an awkward and lanky part-time worker at Gio's Antiques, located in a fictional neighborhood akin to Newark, NJ, in the early '70s, when one day he meets Richard, a suave chain-smoker and auction runner looking to do business with the antique shop. Tired of his lowly position and desperate for some quick cash to help his dying mother, Clive makes a spur-of-the-moment offer to Richard to sell a treasured vanity of rare and coveted design. The sale goes swimmingly at the auction, until a competitor of Richard's reveals the vanity is a fake. Clive and Richard will now owe millions to the buyers and auction club that will soon hunt them down. Richard knows of only one organization they could possibly turn to: the local Mafia. But can Clive survive—and maybe even find unexpected solace—among the sharks in Richard's gang?

For readers of Ryan Wick's *Safecracker* and for lovers of *Goodfellas*, this debut sheds light on the unspoken, shady world of antiquing. While electrifying in suspense, *Price to Pay* also exemplifies how one can discover true family within the unlikely bonds that are made through the most trying of circumstances.

I've also received several endorsements from the faculty of the Rutgers University, where I work, and have been interviewed on over 25 true-crime fiction podcasts this past year for my short stories.

The full manuscript is available upon request, but I would be delighted to send a few sample chapters, should that be best for your consideration!

My best,
Jules Eve C.

Knowing the elements that agents actually want in a query letter puts you miles beyond most aspiring writers out there hoping to get an agent. Now it's time to decide who to target with your pitch. Read on to the last step to discover how to research, woo, and secure the ideal agent to represent you.

POST PITCH

Find
Your Agent

Dear Writer,
Let's talk!
—LUCINDA

When Tracy McCubbin's pitch, featured in the last chapter, landed on my desk, I was initially resistant. As a highly successful entrepreneur with celebrity clientele, Tracy had plenty of credibility, but she didn't have the visible online platform that editors would need to see in the competitive category of decluttering. I worried this would be too tough a sell.

I told her as much over e-mail. She responded with a phone call: "Lucinda, I know I'm not a big name, but I'm going to make this a huge success. It's going to be as big as Marie Kondo. I have a whole series in mind. I'm flying up to New York to meet with agents, and I'd love for you to be one of them."

Tracy is a Crusader through and through. Sure enough, Tracy's query letter had garnered enough interest to land her multiple interviews with small and big agencies alike. Though I was still skeptical, I had to admit I was now intrigued. When agents line up for a pageant, it tends to signal the market will respond positively too. More than that, Tracy had vision, and she was prepared to launch not just one book but an entire career.

We met a few days later at my office. Fresh off a flight from Los Angeles, Tracy requested an almond milk latte from my assistant and was met with a blank stare. But Tracy wasn't typical Hollywood. She had come prepared with the analysis of the Data Collector. She had evidence of the success of her process in the form of hundreds of clients she had helped, frustrated that mainstream advice had failed them. In her high-energy, animated way, she pointed out gaps in the Marie Kondo method that she had learned through her experience in business for over a decade. Her clients were struggling, and it wasn't just them: America's clutter epidemic was urgent—economically, environmentally, and psychologically.

Since she was meeting with other agents, she asked me what I brought to the table and why I would be the right advocate for her, what kinds of publishers I saw for the book, and what books I had represented that looked like hers. These aren't the questions of an amateur. An expert knows that the authority shifts when you control the interview and are no longer the person being interviewed. It turns out agents, much like editors, want a chance to prove their mettle too.

BEST PRACTICES FOR RESEARCHING AGENTS

It's time to take your perfect pitch and send it out into the world. But how do you find the right agents? Most people start with the Internet. This can be deceptively helpful, especially after you identify a name or two and visit their agency website to learn more. But then you find 20 agents who seem like they could be a fit. Then 50 more. Then 100. Unfortunately, many of the free lists of literary agents have outdated information. Google is as questionable a resource for your medical issue as it is your future publishing partner. It's no wonder so many writers get nowhere finding agents this way, and if you haven't started yet, I hope I can save you from that probable way right to someone's slush pile. There's a reason it's called that! But there's no reason that the book you've worked so hard on should ever be considered slush.

Here are some more effective shortcuts.

Tap a published author friend if you have one.
While it would be terrific to have an author friend who has published a similar book, take advantage of *any* connection you have with any literary agent or publisher who is willing to read a brief e-mail about your book or take a 15-minute call with you. Most agencies, Lucinda Literary being no exception, are in the business of referrals. Any agent will take a referral or personal introduction more seriously than a query submitted blindly. This is one reason why building that network we talked about in Step 5 is so important. If you have made strategic and authentic connections to others in your niche, there is a good chance you know a published author with an agent. Ask them for an introduction—an introduction is everything.

Read the acknowledgments section of books in your genre(s).
This is advice you may have heard. It's obvious but
worth repeating. Writers should be well versed in the
works of their peers, bearing a strong grasp of what readers in their genre want to read. Read the acknowledgments
of recent favorite books that inspired you—an agent is
usually acknowledged. That is how Ron Friedman developed his original, extensive agent spreadsheet. You can
then approach the agent with a personalized note in your
pitch, conveying that you are actually familiar with their
authors. If you're thinking of mentioning just one big hit,
I'd suggest adding a lesser-known title.

Pitch more junior agents at a marquis agency.
Writers frequently ask if they should query a very seasoned agent or a newbie. There's no one answer; it's more
about the research you do and the personal connection
you feel if you ultimately have correspondence with that
person. I will say this: a junior or assistant agent with over
three years of experience at a respected agency is probably
in it for the long haul, has been trained by someone with
industry expertise and strong relationships, and is hungry
to build a list. If you're fortunate enough to get an interview, you may be meeting a rising star.

*Use Publishers Marketplace, Manuscript Wish List, or a
similar industry database.*
Publishers Marketplace offers a free daily newsletter
with recent deals and a paid subscription that gives you
access to a wide database of current publishing contacts,
the deals they've done, and their personal contact information. Having even a direct e-mail address to an agent
can make all the difference in getting your query letter
seen by the right person. Here you can easily find who

represents similar authors to you and what kinds of publishers and editors they make deals with. Like searching the acknowledgments, PM and other databases are gold mines of agent names to collect.

Take advantage of social media.

Using LinkedIn, X (formerly Twitter), or Instagram is today's means of following an agent's work and interests and allows you to contact someone directly with a very brief pitch or a quick hook into a conversation. What social media offers, which an endless online Rolodex will not, is a glimpse into an agent or publisher's personal interests and world.

Interns and assistants are often the first gatekeepers, and they are a lot easier to connect with online. I encourage new writers to connect with the assistants of their dream agents on LinkedIn or follow them on social media. Engage with these people, get to know their personalities or interests as a way of running up the flagpole. When you finally pitch them, you want them to recognize your name.

Attend the events where agents are.

More than likely, your agent is being interviewed on somebody's podcast, quoted in an article about industry trends, spearheading their own projects online, or attending conferences. The agent that you want representing you is actively being sought after by industry professionals hoping to harness some of their insights. What better way to connect with them than by attending one of the many lectures, workshops, and other—increasingly virtual— events where they speak, where you can ask them questions directly? Showing up lets them know that you are serious. Hopefully it creates name recognition and eventually a relationship. I've formed a number of relationships with attendees of our classes and coaching and rooted from the sidelines as they got signed.

Ideally, your future agent will have experience representing books similar to yours and authors whose careers you admire. Perhaps these agents have worked with your dream publishers. But the most important qualification should be true enthusiasm for you and your book. I think Lucy Carson, senior agent at The Friedrich Agency, put it best: "I actually believe in my heart of hearts that individuals are where the difference is made. Don't make your decision on the basis of how big a company is. You're signing with a human being. And if you love a human being in a big, small, or medium-sized agency, you'll be fine."

RETHINK YOUR SUBMISSION APPROACH

I am always dismayed to hear when a writer has queried 50 agents at once and saddened when these efforts yield no response. This happens far too often, and there is a more methodical, effective approach for securing the right attention. But it requires keeping your own urgency at bay.

Conduct solid research and query agents who are right for your project, again personalizing each letter early in your query. If it is your very first time querying agents and you are uncertain that your pitch is quite where it needs to be, go to a small list of 10 to 12 agents first. If you elicit a quick reply and feel confident in your pitch, go to the next 5 to 10 agents you have researched. This approach of "querying in rounds" is one that we often use at Lucinda Literary when approaching editors—seeking market feedback and then adopting the actual language we hear as we continue our pitching efforts. These adoptions can be anything from highlighting a novel's strengths to rebutting reservations which we now expect will be an issue for others. While beauty is in the eye of the beholder, industry insiders do share common sensibilities. When you can begin to detect a trend to the criticism, you know that you have useful data.

One novelist named Lindsay, who I worked with at the outset of my career, did this beautifully. She originally arrived in my inbox with obvious energy on the page and a memoir about her time working in the beauty industry à la *The Devil Wears Prada*. I suggested that she recast her memoir as fiction to allow for more poetic liberties—with characters, plot, and the drama that makes for great books-to-film. She took the feedback on board, revised her pitch and manuscript accordingly, and returned to me one year later with a competitive offer in hand.

Query a mix of big agencies, boutique agencies, and solo agents. There are drawbacks and benefits to all of these. Big agencies bring more staff and resources. Boutiques and solo agents typically service a smaller volume of clients and can offer authors more individual attention. It's important to have this diversity in who you approach, not yet knowing where your potential will be seen. You might have your heart set on someone you admire from afar, but it turns out that it could be someone entirely different who falls in love with your work, is willing to build your career with you, and will therefore be a better advocate.

Here is another question I am asked all the time: *What will a positive response look like?* Consider any response that's not "no" positive because you have achieved the goal of the query: to get in conversation with an agent. There is so much more you can expand upon and convince them of once you get them face-to-face. Even then, if they do say no, it's not always the end of the line. You can still follow up in a way that keeps the door open.

For now, here is one of your most important take-aways: if you aren't getting a reply to your e-mail, there's a problem with your pitch. If you receive a positive response to your pitch but then the line goes dead, the issue likely lies with the material.

If you receive a number of manuscript requests, enthusiastic reviews, or even suggestions of offers of representation, you may consider widening your submission list to include even more agents, hopeful for as many agent offers as possible. Agents find themselves in this chair as well, facing the decision to keep a list small or go wide. There isn't a science behind any particular strategy that I can lend to you; you will need to find the one that suits you. It's entirely normal to have conversations with several agents, and it is also just as normal to trust your instincts and know right away. (When I interview authors, I do!)

WHEN YOU'RE NOT GETTING A RESPONSE

Even if you've done the research, your query letter is strong, and the agents you have contacted are a good fit, there is a good chance you will not hear back from several people. Beware the spam filter! Even if your e-mail *is* landing, or you're submitting through an online portal, our inboxes see multiple queries every day and possibly up to roughly 100 per week. Yikes.

This makes the answer to "Should I follow up if I don't hear back?" an easy one. Unless an agency sternly prohibits this approach, there isn't harm in summoning your inner Crusader, your future self who doesn't take silence for an answer. Pursue the one you want. If you do choose to follow up, think strategically and act concisely. You could even follow up with an assistant or a direct e-mail address if you first used a form and are afraid of appearing too pushy. It is difficult to not receive any word at all on the work you have belabored on for months or even years. It's worth taking a second shot.

A simple "confirming this e-mail arrived" about a month after you've sent a query can ensure it was received in the first place. If I'm seeing an intriguing query for the first time, I'll ask my office to pull its history.

But there are even more productive ways to follow up with agents. Here are some strategies:

- Congratulate an agent on a recent publication or recently announced deal. This would not only be kind but impressive that you are following their career.

- Point to breakout or best-selling comps, recent news events, or trends that suggest your topic is timely.

- Share that a notable podcast, journal, or press outlet has just featured your story.

- Entice the agent with a pre-existing endorsement of your work, research, or anything else about you from a well-known author or influencer. This isn't necessarily the blurb that will go on the book jacket. It simply shows us that you have legitimate connections and respect in your area of expertise.

- Send an update that you have had multiple requests for your proposal or manuscript, received with enthusiastic reads.

And if you have offers from other agents, or even if you're scheduling actual interviews (never lie; it's a small world where people talk), now we're really paying attention. What you're aiming for in your follow-up is to give the impression that something is *happening*. In this way, a query that missed us the first time around is more likely to get through to us the second time. I never recommend a passive approach once a respectful amount of time has passed. It's too easy to get lost in the crowd.

As agents, we use these tactics every day when we're querying editors, and here's the thing: the worst you can hear is no. I think that's better than silence. What do you really have to lose when the stakes are so high?

If after you follow up, you don't hear from the agent you've queried, it's time to move on. Not every agent is for you, and that's okay. There are many possible reasons why an agent won't respond, and it may be entirely unrelated to you—a full pipeline, a client emergency to deal with, a family member being ill. It's not productive for you to spend your time guessing. Time to go back out and find the right person. Their loss!

INTERPRETING AGENT SPEAK

Sometimes an agent will review your query and give you a negative response, and sometimes that can be accompanied by a vague or unhelpful reason. This is especially applicable if, in the agency's query guidelines, you were asked to share an excerpt or proposal. A few examples include:

"Your platform is too small."

"I didn't connect with the voice."

"The field is too crowded."

"This doesn't fit with my list."

"I'm not accepting new clients."

"I'm not the agent for this project."

"I don't have the right relationships to see this through."

"I found myself yearning for a stronger setup."

These responses typically boil down to the three keys we discussed in Step 1: idea, writing, or platform. And if you receive a rejection, gather your courage, step into your writer type, and try to find out which keys were missing.

Crusaders are inspired by rejection. But whether you matched to this type, there is a thread to pull. And there is no harm if you politely inquire if there's a comment you don't understand. At worst, you will hear nothing back. At best, very specific questions will elicit single or multiple choice answers that will guide improvements to your pitch from there. Here's what I would ask if I were in your shoes:

- "Can I trouble you to tell me what you didn't find sellable?" (This is always a great one to ask if they haven't pointed to a reason for declining.)

- "I appreciate your candor. It would be so helpful if you could tell me where you lost interest."

- "I understand the platform is modest; was there also an issue with the writing or idea?" (I like this one because it points to the three keys. You may only have one, and you need at least one of the other two.)

- "I appreciate that you didn't find the idea original or novel enough to break through. Was there also an issue in my social media following, or was this irrelevant to your consideration?" (As above, you're trying to deduce which, if any, of the keys were missing.)

- Another leading multiple-choice question could look like this: "Was it the idea, writing, platform, or something else?"

It never fails to amaze (and enlighten) me when a host of editors pick up on a weakness I hadn't even seen. They are my trusted psychics, because that weakness we antici-pated as agents or heard back from editors often plays out in prime time when a book is being pitched to the media or is getting reactions from readers.

In the same way, negative feedback from an agent can be the greatest gift you never expected.

The main takeaway is if you receive *any* kind of response from an agent, consider responding with a thank-you or a brief clarifying question following the above examples. This is about establishing conversation and rapport. If you are thoughtful in your correspondence, an agent will remember you down the line.

INTERVIEWING AND SELECTING AN AGENT

If you keep honing your strengths as a writer and cali-brating your idea or your platform based on the feedback you receive, you will succeed in finding your agent. In this book I've already mentioned people like Lindsay and Chris who took feedback I offered. The editors and agents

I interviewed have similar stories. In fact, when we give feedback at all, it's a positive sign. One day, and it may not be far, you will receive interest in your work.

You know you're on the track to getting signed when you receive an effusive letter from an agent, but a promising response can also be as simple as: "Michelle, I really loved your proposal, and I have some additions to recommend if you're interested in discussing. Could we schedule a call in the next few weeks?"

Most often this agent will have read your full proposal or manuscript, but in the nonfiction genre, frequently a pitch is all we need to know that it's going to be a "hot" project—typically one where the author is well established as an expert, journalist, or leader in their field and is likely to get snatched up quickly. In those instances, we'll want to set up a meeting right away. The interview is like a blind date. You've Googled one another, but you have no idea whether there will be chemistry.

How to Prep for Your First Meeting

During that first conversation with an agent, you will be asked a number of questions like:

- "Why do you want to write this book?"
- "Why are you the person to write it?"
- "Who is your target reader?"
- "What should I know about your platform?"

Do these sound familiar? They should! These are the exact questions you have spent the better part of this book answering, so you've already done the prep. But, as with any good relationship, you're looking to make sure the agent is a good fit for you too, so come prepared to ask questions like the ones below.

- "What appealed to you most about my book?"
- "What challenges in the market do you see for my kind of book?"
- "What books have you had the most success with?"
- "How long do you estimate the development and submission process would take?"
- "What kinds of publishers would you approach for this book?"
- "Do you have relationships with these publishers?"
- "I want to impress upon you that I'm willing to do whatever it takes both to write and promote this book. What do you see as essential to revise?"
- "What's your preferred working style with authors?"
- "Would you be my primary point person, or would I ever be dealing with someone else?"
- "What happens if we don't get a deal?"
- "I want this partnership to be successful for you. What are the qualities of the kinds of clients you enjoy working with?"

In addition to asking the questions above, here are some quick tips on how to be irresistible in your conversations with agents:

- Express gratitude and exhibit research of the agent or publisher's books or website.

- Demonstrate how well read or well connected you are in your category.

- Get the pitch for your book down to a simple, memorable sentence or two.

- Paint a picture of your audience, what they crave, and what they ask you for.

- Reference your vision and promotional plans for the book.

- Make sure to keep the conversation interactive; listen first and try not to overtalk when you answer.

- Ask about next steps.

What to Look For in an Agent

During those first few interactions, there are several qualities you'll want to evaluate.

1. Someone who shares your editorial vision and passion for the book's success. This is the most important factor.

2. Someone with honesty and integrity.

3. Someone who can be a strong business advocate for you. This can come down to an agent's experience overseeing successful books in a similar genre or the kind of sales track record or publisher relationships she has. But not always. Remember that a newer agent might be a great partner. Sometimes

the less-experienced rising star is exactly the right person who will be most industrious and dedicated.

4.   Someone who will bring out the best in you. You may strive to be a stronger writer or more seriously regarded as one, seek guidance in marketing, or simply need someone to relieve your anxiety and make you laugh all while keeping you focused on the big picture and not the small distractions. It's wise to enter the room knowing what you need most, stating it up front, and assessing whether the agent is best suited to help.

If there's one key takeaway, it's to try to gauge the balance of whether this person can bring your work to its full potential and market value combined with: Will this person be with you when the going gets tough? In choosing an independent agent from out of several options, best-selling thriller writer Lisa Unger asked: "If we don't sell my book, will you still be my agent?" "Yes," her agent answered, "because you're going to have a career."

Red Flags to Look Out For in Agents

An agent who will not edit your proposal or manuscript, takes weeks to respond, or, in juggling a large client load, is likely to slow down the process.

To us, this is a big red flag for a project—reputable publishers are unlikely to welcome new material that doesn't have an expert's fingertips on it. My favorite part of the job (besides the auction!) is the "all-in" day-and-night engagement with my writers to create the biggest idea, the drop-dead title, and the book proposal that editors will put down everything else to read. And if an agent takes you on, they should be working with urgency because the market for any book is moving fast. Ask about their timeline.

An agent who overpromises money, celebrity connections, a film deal, or a New York Times bestseller.

There are no guarantees as to how the market will respond to your work. Nothing is guaranteed! The best client representatives under-promise and over-deliver.

An agent or publisher who hasn't had any experience with your book's genre or seems ill-equipped to advise you on business matters.

If you're speaking with someone new to the industry, you need to be really convinced of that person's vision, relationships, and the kind of mentoring they will be receiving along the way.

Your gut instinct tells you something is not right.

Trust it! And don't hesitate to ask for a reference and/or an attorney's review of the client agreement you receive.

What Does Your Agent Expect from You?

Imagine the interview passed muster and everyone left excited. The next step is for an agent to offer representation, typically by way of an informal e-mail or during your discussion. Should you accept, you will sign a contract and enter into a legal agreement. As a long-term, binding agreement, it's important to understand every word and to ensure that each term is industry standard or that there's a credible explanation if it isn't. If you aren't planning to engage an attorney, many others turn to the Authors Guild website as a resource.

Then it's time to pop the champagne and tell your friends, because you've gotten signed with a literary agent! A book deal may not be far from view. To keep the relationship smooth and productive, here's a sense of what an agent might expect of you:

Welcome transparency.

This is far and away the most important thing you can do right off the bat. Be honest about everything: who you are, your goals, what you expect, etc. To call upon the marriage analogy once again, it's not recommended to keep secrets we'll find out later. Tell us everything we need to know that may come up about you—discuss any negatives that are googleable and tell us anything that isn't. Have you published before with dismal sales numbers? Been involved in a nasty lawsuit? Have you already been represented? Better to be forthright. An experienced agent will either strategize with you or know a way to get out in front of these challenges.

Know what you don't know.

You are the expert on your idea and your story. You are not an expert on the business of book publishing. When I met Jayne, she was successfully self-published, and a publisher, noting her success, had offered her a contract. She was torn. It was a good offer but not the one she wanted. I intuited we could get a better offer from one of the Big Five, and I asked her to trust her gut and mine. We turned down the other publisher and took a leap of faith together as we submitted her book to a curated list of publishers that I knew would be interested in her fresh topic and voice. When she received a four-book deal from HarperCollins, her trust in the relationship paid off. There's never a guarantee, but if you do what you do best, it allows us to do what we do best.

Push back when there's something you do know.

One of my favorite traits in an author is when they educate *me* and make me rethink a point of critique. If you receive any sort of editorial feedback from an agent that you feel firmly will not resonate with your audience or feels out of sync with what you're looking to create, make the case and express understanding, but stand strong. Agents work for you; we're here to improve your work based on what we believe the market wants. We're not always correct. Often there's a compromise to be made between an author's vision and an agent's argument. Far from alienating someone, the experienced agent will view this as a sign of your authority, and it will earn you their respect.

Keep up momentum.

Agenting is a people business. Most agents and editors want to work with people they like! These shared values, combined with a shared editorial vision, should create momentum as you shape your material in partnership with your agent. We sign authors who we see as dedicated to that process and therefore expect you to deliver on feedback or raise an issue without too much time passing. Consistent, reliable, and respectful communication is nonnegotiable.

THE PUBLISHING TIMELINE

After you get signed, there is still work to do to ensure your book proposal or manuscript meets the high standard a traditional publisher expects. We've seen authors shocked that it can happen so fast—within a matter of a few months or even weeks. Other authors may reach a point where they ask themselves, *Will my book ever actually go on submission?* When this happens, Lucinda Literary agent Connor Eck encourages that you think about "the small victories you achieve along the way. Be prepared to work hard. In fact, welcome the rigor."

While no submission will ever be perfect, your agent will tell you when it's ready to go—and if you want to see your project to market sooner, that's always your call to make. Whatever the case, you'll be happy you put in the extra work. Though every journey to a book deal and publication is different, here is a rough timeline of what you can expect.

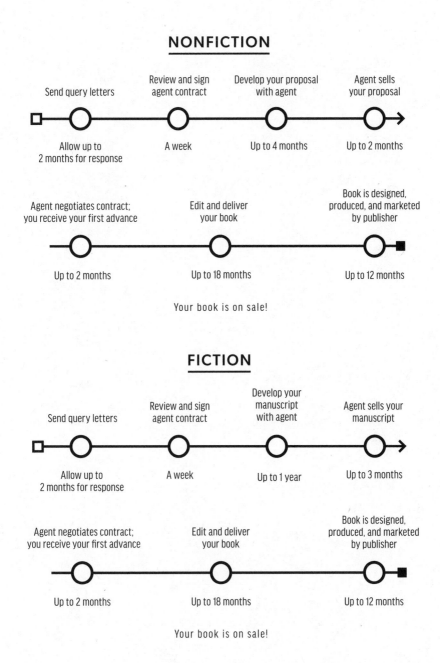

NONFICTION

Send query letters
Allow up to
2 months for response

Review and sign
agent contract
A week

Develop your proposal
with agent
Up to 4 months

Agent sells
your proposal
Up to 2 months

Agent negotiates contract;
you receive your first advance
Up to 2 months

Edit and deliver
your book
Up to 18 months

Book is designed,
produced, and marketed
by publisher
Up to 12 months

Your book is on sale!

FICTION

Send query letters
Allow up to
2 months for response

Review and sign
agent contract
A week

Develop your
manuscript
with agent
Up to 1 year

Agent sells your
manuscript
Up to 3 months

Agent negotiates contract;
you receive your first advance
Up to 2 months

Edit and deliver
your book
Up to 18 months

Book is designed,
produced, and marketed
by publisher
Up to 12 months

Your book is on sale!

CONCLUSION

What's Next for You

One of my favorite stories to tell is that of Dr. Mary Anderson. She was our first student to get signed and get a deal with one of the Big Five. Dr. Mary, as we affectionately call her, came to write a book in the same way many of you probably did: the book she yearned for didn't yet exist.

Mary is a therapist who counsels high-achieving, anxious patients—from overworked physicians and burned-out accountants to successful executives with failing family relationships and even chronically on-edge students. She helps driven, determined individuals who suffer from self-doubt to conquer the cognitive distortions she believes fuel their anxiety. As a result of her work, Mary's patients can find peace of mind without losing their characteristic drive. After years of teaching the same science-based strategies and skills, Mary thought, *There must be a book I can recommend that covers this.* But when she went looking, she couldn't find it. So she decided to write one.

Right away, Mary knew she was out of her comfort zone. She understood very little about the book writing process and worried, as a high-achiever herself, that she would fall short of her own and others' expectations. Fortunately, through a series of happy introductions that she likened to "Dorothy walking down the yellow brick road," she ended up in my online master class Get Signed.

Little by little, Mary walked through the process outlined in this book, focusing on the three keys: 1) a big and bold idea, 2) excellent writing, and 3) an undeniable platform.

She sharpened her big idea—that many people at the peaks of their careers or domains have different challenges and therefore require different solutions. She understood the gap her book filled in the marketplace. And while many self-help books have been written for those with anxiety, there wasn't one in existence targeted to high-achievers specifically, especially at a moment when mental health disorders were skyrocketing.

With practice, Mary grew confident in her elevator pitch and became laser-focused on the audience she could help. She began to experiment with social media, speaking, and writing for publications. She thoughtfully crafted a website that would present her as an accomplished practitioner but also a teacher—one who might just as easily become your best friend. All the while, young in her career, she battled imposter syndrome and the act of putting herself before the public eye. But "if the price of admission to do great things is my own vulnerability," Mary said, "I'm willing to pay that to help as many people as possible."

Mary then set to work on writing her query letter, the one she had once been terrified to write, which now came more easily after deeply understanding the mission and value behind it. But then she was sidetracked by unexpected life events, something that all writers are prone to experience. Mary's father died, and instead of taking an important meeting she had planned for her book, she found herself on a plane halfway across the country to attend his funeral. When she returned, she was still recovering from her loss. But she didn't lose sight of her dream to get published. It was something her father had always encouraged her to pursue, and now it became as much a part of his legacy as hers.

Mary put her perfectionism aside, braced for critique, and when she received it, she recalibrated. After several rounds of feedback, she felt her query letter was ready. It wasn't long before she landed an agent and then eventually the book deal that seemed possible only in her wildest dreams.

Translated into multiple languages, with a television show in view, Mary's book has created the speaking and writing career she always wanted, distinguishing her business and helping many more people globally than her local client practice ever could. There are plenty of mediums that can scale your message, but only one can stand the test of time, lending permanence to your story or claim. And just as it can change the lives of others, a book can, as it did for Mary, change your life's trajectory.

In these pages, you have learned about what it takes to get signed by a literary agent. That is no small task, and I'll be tremendously proud of anyone who is now able to find the publishing partner of their dreams. (I hope to hear from you!) But your agent is just one person in the village you've built—the one who took you under their wing, ushered you through the door, and introduced you to all the other people you should know.

You will remember where you were standing, the time of day, and even what the sky, the trees, and the light looked like when you answered the phone from your agent to receive your first book offer. This is just the beginning of the true metamorphosis. It may lead to a rewarding new company, a social media brand, a film, a community, or a nonprofit initiative. Once you have crystallized your unique offering in connection to the wider world, you will be more confident in your success, whichever route you choose.

Will you take the leap?

GLOSSARY

Advance: This is the guaranteed payment a publisher will invest when they agree to buy the rights to your book. Your agent will negotiate your advance on your behalf. It is usually split into installments paid out over several years' time, based on milestones like contract signing, acceptance of the manuscript, and publication.

Backlist: Previously published titles from an author, publisher, or agency, different from the author's newest work, known as the "frontlist."

Big Five: The five largest publishing houses: currently Penguin Random House, Simon & Schuster, Macmillan, HarperCollins, and Hachette Book Group. Publishers outside of these five houses are referred to as independent, or "indie," publishers.

Blurb: A short quote praising your book from someone of prominence or an expert in the author's field. You'll often see blurbs in book descriptions online or on the book jacket.

Book Proposal: Typically required for nonfiction writers to sell their book. A proposal generally consists of 20 to 50 pages that include a book overview, table of contents, chapter summaries, sample chapters, an author bio, and a marketing/platform section.

Comparative Titles/"Comps": Books (or other forms of media) that are similar to your own in genre, writing style, audience, or content.

Editor: A person working on behalf of a publishing house who is responsible for editing your book before it is produced. An editor will typically collaborate with you on major revisions, and also line edit your work. Many editors acquire books, which means they agree to buy it on behalf of the publisher before they begin the editing process. They are your champions "in house."

Frontlist: Newly published titles from a publisher or agency within the first year of publication.

Hybrid Publishing: A mix between traditional and self-publishing, where authors do not receive an advance and are required to pay for their books in exchange for editing, design, production, marketing, and distribution services.

Imprint: A division within a larger publishing company that specializes in a specific type of book or certain genres. The larger publishing companies have dozens of imprints that differ in ethos and acquisitions taste.

List: A colloquial term for the roster of books that an agent represents or that an editor has acquired.

Manuscript: The document that contains the text of your book (and any illustrations) before it is edited.

Material: Your writing, in whole or part. For works of fiction, your material is your manuscript. For nonfiction, it can be your book proposal or your manuscript.

Platform: Your online or professional presence, defined in this book as "audience + reach." This can refer to social media but also to publications you have written for, speaking appearances, a teaching affiliation, graduate degrees, your network, and more. Your platform represents your public recognition and is viewed from the lens of impacting prospective book sales. Platform is covered extensively in Step 5.

Profit and Loss Statement/P&L: Editors will put together a P&L in order to determine if a book is worth publishing based on its expected sales (profits) versus its expenses (losses). The comps you provide for your book, along with those an editor determines, can help publishers project how profitable your book will be.

Publishers Marketplace: A website that contains a database of publishing deals, a directory of industry contacts, and a newsletter that provides daily industry news.

Royalties: The share belonging to an author when book sales exceed the initial advance. These are paid in perpetuity, so long as a book remains in print. Agents help negotiate these percentages during the signing process. If an author has entered into a flat fee agreement, they are not entitled to royalties.

Slush Pile/"Slush": Unsolicited manuscripts and book proposals that gather in an agent or publisher's inbox.

Submission: The process of submitting a pitch, and a manuscript or proposal to editors at publishing houses.

Submission List: The curated list of editors to whom your agent chooses to pitch your work.

Trade Press/Trade Publisher: Publishing houses that create and distribute books for the general reading market and wide public consumption through bookstores and online retail. Trade presses do not publish academic books or textbooks.

ENDNOTES

1. Gina Nicoll, "Why Is *The Body Keeps the Score* So Popular Right Now?," *Book Riot*, October 15, 2021, https://bookriot.com/the-body-keeps-the-score-popularity/.

2. Danny McLoughlin, "Amazon Book Sales Statistics," WordsRated, November 9, 2022, https://wordsrated.com/amazon-book-sales-statistics/.

3. "7 Star Read," n.d., https://www.amazon.com/product-reviews/0593441273/ref=cm_cr_getr_d_paging_btm_next_2?ie=UTF8&filterByStar=five_star&reviewerType=all_reviews&pageNumber=2#reviews-filter-bar.

4. Paula Cocozza, "A New Start After 60," *The Guardian*, updated August 27, 2021, https://www.theguardian.com/lifeandstyle/2021/aug/27/a-new-start-after-60-anne-youngson-meet-me-at-the-museum.

5. Catherine Baab-Muguira, "The Query Letter That Got Me Four Agent Offers," *Poe Can Save Your Life*, March 19, 2022, https://poecansaveyourlife.substack.com/p/the-query-letter-that-got-me-four.

ACKNOWLEDGMENTS

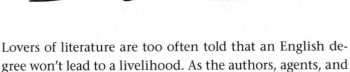

Lovers of literature are too often told that an English degree won't lead to a livelihood. As the authors, agents, and editors in this book prove, that's an erroneous assumption. So I want to begin by thanking the educators who encouraged us bookish people to pursue the meaningful work of ushering new writing into the world. The world can't turn without a rubric for understanding it.

My deepest gratitude lies with the authors who placed their trust in me. You are my teachers and muses, the reason I'm in the position to write this book in the first place. Certain clients among you—Ron Friedman, Susan Peirce Thompson, Rishon Blumberg, Chris Bailey, Jayne Allen, Ann Shoket, Paul Jarvis, Nicola Kraus, and Cait Flanders—have gone above and beyond to lend your wisdom to this book and even your counsel in making it a success.

The editors, agents, and authors who contributed to this book—Tracy Sherrod, Jenny Jackson, Stephanie Frerich, Rick Kot, Paul Whitlatch, Michelle Howry, Sarah Pelz, Alex Littlefield, Jane Friedman, Lucy Carson, Byrd Leavell, Alex Glass, Mark Fortier, Adam Grant, Chris Bailey, Peter Heller, Mike Michalowicz, Asha Frost, Colette Baron-Reid, Ben Hardy, Lisa Unger—were gracious in sharing their time and expertise to help me demystify the publishing industry for readers. Editors have a preternatural way of giving language to our thoughts better than we can ourselves.

There's one agent I admire most, and he happens to be my husband, David Halpern. David brings integrity to the job of literary representation as he does with all things in life. His guidance and support when I began Lucinda Literary, on top of his care for our family, has allowed me to fearlessly follow my curiosity and take the leaps of faith I'm wont to do. This book is a stunning example of what's possible when you have a partner like David, one of the last true gentlemen there are.

I always smile when I imagine what my young daughters will envision when they're older, when they ask what Daddy and I did for a living. "So a book auction . . . is that like a bunch of publishers in a room and an auctioneer with a gavel calling out bids?" Olivia and Grace, your peering eyes and tiny giggles sustained me through this mammoth project. I hope that by the time you're older, if you're starting out as professionals yourselves, it will be common to give yourself wholeheartedly to the career you love, without apology.

In this book, I write about how important it is to emulate those you admire, while giving your work its own unique twist. It's no different for any career. Three women shaped me early in my profession: Dee Dee DeBartlo at HarperCollins, Bernadette Grey at Scholastic, and Christy Fletcher at Fletcher & Co, now United Talent Agency. You modeled for me that, particularly as mothers, you could have a fulfilling life and a business. You took a chance on a bratty New York kid and saw the hustle in me.

Liz Morrow—you never failed to awe me with your professionalism, work ethic, and unflagging positive energy. How lucky authors are to work with you as a thought and editing partner.

Lisa Sweetingham—you godsend, you. Why you were inclined to lend your time and brilliance in the early stages and in the final pass, I'll never know. I guess it's because you're family.

Lisa Cheng—thank you for putting me in my place and treating me just as you do our shared authors, with sensitivity and care. Your e-mails were as good as your line edits. I relished our clashing of the minds, and the book is better for your gracious honesty. Monica O'Connor, Tricia Breidenthal, what gems you are!

Patty Gift—there's a reason every Hay House author considers you a best friend. You are uncannily good at what you do. You've taught me that one doesn't always need to steer the ship. Sometimes people can just walk into your life, believe in you, and gift you opportunities you hadn't seen coming.

For Lucinda Literary alumni, the students who have taken our classes—your curiosity and determination made this whole new experience of educating and presenting more rewarding than I ever imagined. Witnessing your successes is the true reason this book was born.

Kelly Notaras and Ashley Bernardi—my masterminds! How grateful I am to have two kick-ass female business owners guide me through twisty situations and cheer me on with every undertaking. Jen Halpern, with your psychic ability and relentless encouragement despite my naysaying every step of the way, you foresaw early on that I would find a calling in writing and teaching. All of you are sisters. (Don't worry, Adare Yanagihara, we know you are my actual sister. And since we were little girls, the way you have believed I could do anything, the way you uplift everyone in your orbit, has been vital to rising to this challenge, among others.)

Lucinda Literary team—and especially Connor Eck, my right-hand, trusted editor and friend, who has "kept the ball rolling" from the earliest days of our agency; Julia Collucci, who, much to the surprise of us both, built a whole online education division with me from the ground up, and whose talent and belief in what we were creating for writers kept me going; Grace Garrahan, our resident "art director," who pitched in with full force; and the team of interns, namely Claire Callahan, who suddenly found themselves reviewing their boss's work (no pressure at all)—I am not worthy! I am blessed.

You've all made it possible for me to step with confidence into my future self.

Writers, it's your time now.

ABOUT THE AUTHOR

Lucinda Halpern is a literary agent with nearly 20 years' experience in both the publicity and agency sides of publishing. Before founding Lucinda Literary, she worked in the publicity division of HarperCollins, where she assisted on the media campaign for *Freakonomics*, among other *New York Times* bestsellers. She later took a management role in sales and marketing at Scholastic before launching her career as an agent. She has worked with such publishers as HarperCollins, Penguin Random House, Simon & Schuster, Macmillan, and Hachette, and currently represents *New York Times* and internationally best-selling authors in the categories of business, health, lifestyle, popular science, narrative nonfiction, memoir, and upmarket fiction. You can find her online at **lucindaliterary.com** and **getsignedbook.com**.

Hay House Titles of Related Interest

THE SHIFT, the movie,
starring Dr. Wayne W. Dyer
(available as an online streaming video)
www.hayhouse.com/the-shift-movie

• • •

HIGH PERFORMANCE HABITS:
How Extraordinary People Become That Way,
by Brendon Burchard

THE BOOK YOU WERE BORN TO WRITE: Everything You Need to
(Finally) Get Your Wisdom onto the Page and into the World,
by Kelly Notaras

RISK FORWARD: Embrace the Unknown and
Unlock Your Hidden Genius, by Victoria Labalme

TWO WEEKS NOTICE: Find the Courage to Quit Your Job, Make
More Money, Work Where You Want, and Change the World,
by Amy Porterfield

• • •

All of the above are available at your local bookstore,
or may be ordered by contacting Hay House (see next page).

We hope you enjoyed this Hay House book. If you'd like to receive our online catalog featuring additional information on Hay House books and products, or if you'd like to find out more about the Hay Foundation, please contact:

Hay House, Inc., P.O. Box 5100, Carlsbad, CA 92018-5100
(760) 431-7695 or (800) 654-5126
(760) 431-6948 (fax) or (800) 650-5115 (fax)
www.hayhouse.com® • www.hayfoundation.org

———

Published in Australia by: Hay House Australia Pty. Ltd.,
18/36 Ralph St., Alexandria NSW 2015
Phone: 612-9669-4299 • *Fax:* 612-9669-4144
www.hayhouse.com.au

Published in the United Kingdom by: Hay House UK, Ltd.,
The Sixth Floor, Watson House, 54 Baker Street, London W1U 7BU
Phone: +44 (0)20 3927 7290 • *Fax:* +44 (0)20 3927 7291
www.hayhouse.co.uk

Published in India by: Hay House Publishers India,
Muskaan Complex, Plot No. 3, B-2, Vasant Kunj, New Delhi 110 070
Phone: 91-11-4176-1620 • *Fax:* 91-11-4176-1630
www.hayhouse.co.in

———

Access New Knowledge.
Anytime. Anywhere.

Learn and evolve at your own pace
with the world's leading experts.

www.hayhouseU.com